Advance Praise for
Working Well

"*Working Well* is a powerful reminder that empathy and connection aren't soft skills—they're essential ones. Nidhi blends personal experience and clinical insight to show leaders how attunement can transform both workplaces and people's lives. This book doesn't just teach you how to lead better—it shows you how to see, hear, and support others in ways that create lasting trust and belonging."

—Dr. Marshall Goldsmith, Thinkers50 #1 Executive Coach and *New York Times* bestselling author of *The Earned Life*, *Triggers*, and *What Got You Here Won't Get You There*

"*Working Well* offers much-needed practical guidance on how attunement can help you form genuine connections and boost your well-being at work. It's a must-read for anyone looking to thrive, not just survive, in their professional life."

—Liz Fosslien and Mollie West Duffy, coauthors of *No Hard Feelings* and *Big Feelings*

"If the future of work is human, we need to know how humans work. In *Working Well*, Nidhi Tewari does just that. She bridges the science of connection with practical tools for effective leadership. This book is a road map to healthier and more human-centered workplaces. Highly recommend."

—Britt Frank, LSCSW, author of *The Science of Stuck* and *Align Your Mind*

"An essential read for any working person, from entry level to senior leadership. This book is practical, easily digestible, and loaded with aha moments to help improve working relationships and corporate culture in a meaningful way. This is a refreshing and honest look at the evolution of emotional intelligence into attunement. A must-read for people leaders!"

—Emily Durham, aka @Emily.the.Recruiter, author of *Clock In*

Working Well

How to Build a Happier, Healthier Workplace Through the Science of Attunement

Nidhi Tewari, MSW, LCSW
Foreword by Amy Cuddy

TARCHER
an imprint of Penguin Random House
New York

Tarcher
an imprint of Penguin Random House LLC
1745 Broadway, New York, NY 10019
penguinrandomhouse.com

Most Tarcher books are available at a discount when purchased in quantity for sales promotions or corporate use. Special editions, which include personalized covers, excerpts, and corporate imprints, can be created when purchased in large quantities. For more information, please email specialmarkets@penguinrandomhouse.com. Your local bookstore can also assist with discounted bulk purchases using the Penguin Random House corporate Business-to-Business program. For assistance in locating a participating retailer, email B2B@penguinrandomhouse.com.

Book design by Stephanie Kowalsky, Chocolate Chip Print Media Co.

LIBRARY OF CONGRESS CATALOGING-IN-PUBLICATION DATA
has been applied for.

Hardcover ISBN: 9798217047864
Ebook ISBN: 9798217047871

Printed in the United States of America
1st Printing

The authorized representative in the EU for product safety and compliance is Penguin Random House Ireland, Morrison Chambers, 32 Nassau Street, Dublin D02 YH68, Ireland, https://eu-contact.penguin.ie.

To my lovely Laura:

Ten years of friendship just wasn't enough.

Your journey with brain cancer and my experiences alongside you inspired me to write this book.

I miss you every day and I keep your postcards on my fridge as a daily reminder of the gift of friendship.

Even though you've passed on, you're right here with me, reminding me to get into good trouble.

Contents

Part III

CHECK-IN • 143

Foreword

by Amy Cuddy

SOME BOOKS ASK a lot of you. This one gives more than it asks.

That's one of the many reasons I love it—and one of the many reasons I love and admire Nidhi Tewari.

Working Well is not like other workplace books. It's not cold or corporate. It's not full of jargon or shaming advice. And it's not trying to impress you with how much the author knows. Instead, this book does something far more generous: It meets you where you are.

Whether you're a leader, a teammate, or someone just trying to hold it together while you do your job and live your life, Nidhi understands what that feels like—and she knows what actually helps. She knows that what most of us want is to feel safe enough to speak up, grounded enough to stay present, and connected enough to trust the people around us. And she knows that those things don't happen by accident. They happen when we practice attunement.

Attunement is the skill—really, the art—of being in tune with yourself and others. It's what lets us ask better questions, offer the right kind of support, read the room more accurately, and stay present in hard moments without shutting down. It's what helps us build real trust, not perform it. And it's what lets us stay human in environments that too often push us to disconnect—from our emotions, from our needs, and from one another.

I first got to know Nidhi during the pandemic, in those surreal months when many of us were holding space for each other through headphones and phone screens. We met on Clubhouse, where we ended up cohosting rooms about mental health, leadership, burnout, grief, trauma—conversations that felt both expansive and intimate. They weren't curated or rehearsed; they were raw and real, and people came to them not for advice, but for truth. And Nidhi showed up again and again with clarity, humility, and so much heart.

She didn't need to be the loudest voice in the room—she was the one people leaned in to hear. The one who could name the thing no one else was saying. The one who could calm a room without softening the truth. She shared her clinical expertise with total generosity, never speaking at people, always with them. And the people in those rooms—myself included—felt seen. Felt safer.

Over time, that connection moved offline. We became real-life friends—colleagues who could go to each other for research and practical guidance, for gut checks, for the hard-to-name questions that come up when you're writing and speaking and trying to make something meaningful out of what you've lived. And what's stayed true in every context—whether it's a group panel, a one-on-one call, or a quick exchange about a talk—is that Nidhi is exactly who she is. There's no mask. No performance. Just a deep commitment to truth, care, and clarity. That's why I trust her, and that's why I trust this book.

I've spent most of my adult life studying power, trust, and presence. I've taught at business schools, spoken to thousands of leaders and organizations, and written books about what happens when we shrink or disappear under pressure—and how we come back into our own. Again and again, I've found myself returning to the same truth: we don't just want to be seen. We need to be felt. And we thrive when we feel in sync—with our bodies, our values, our purpose, and with the people around us.

That's why this book is so important. And that's why Nidhi is the person to write it.

She's not just wise or well-trained—though she is both of those things. She's someone who embodies attunement in every part of her life. On calls where no one has their camera on, she still picks up on who's struggling. She leads with care, even when a firm boundary is required. She expects a lot—of herself, of others—but she holds that standard with grace and spaciousness. She gives people room to grow. And perhaps most importantly: She makes all of this feel possible.

This book isn't overwhelming. You won't walk away with a two-hundred-item checklist of things to fix about yourself. You won't be asked to become someone else. In fact, one of Nidhi's great gifts is that she shows you how to be more of who you already are—just a bit more attuned, a bit more grounded, a bit more clear and kind and steady.

The tools in *Working Well* are practical, research-based,

and immediately useful. But more than that, they're offered with so much humanity. That matters. We learn best when we feel safe. We grow most when we're not being judged. And we're more likely to show up for others when we've been met with real presence ourselves.

I seek attunement in every part of my life—in the classroom, on stage, with my readers, with my husband and son, with my friends, while roller-skating by the ocean, while dancing with others to live music. That sense of being connected—not just to each other, but to the moment, to ourselves, to something bigger—that's what we're wired for. That's what makes us feel alive.

That's also why I find *Working Well* to be such a meaningful companion to my own work on adult bullying, bystanding, and social bravery. My forthcoming book takes on an urgent cultural crisis—the widespread normalization of cruelty, institutional betrayal, and eroded trust in adult life. It maps the systems that allow bullying to thrive, and it offers a framework for helping bystanders become what I call "bravehearts." What Nidhi offers here supports that work in a vital way: by helping people build the relational and emotional muscles they need to notice harm, stay present, respond with care, and repair when needed. It's not just about preventing harm—it's about cultivating the conditions that make courage possible.

Working Well is the book I want to hand to every manager, every team member, every teacher, every person who's ever asked, "Why does this feel so hard?" or "Why doesn't anyone seem to care?" or "How do I help without overstepping?" It's also the book I'd hand to someone who says, "I don't read business books" or "I don't have time for leadership theory." This book will meet them gently, usefully, and with warmth. It will move them forward.

We need a culture shift in how we work and live together. And we won't get there by muscling through. We'll get there through attunement.

Let Nidhi show you how.

Amy Cuddy

Introduction

From Discord to Harmony

Imagine this:

One of your coworkers consistently shows up twenty minutes late to work every day. They are falling behind on their assignments, missing scheduled meetings, and spending more time talking with their colleagues than before. Their bandwidth is low, and they are unable to help the team by stepping in. Colleagues and bosses are having to cover their work for them.

They are doing the bare minimum.

What do you think of this employee? What assumptions have you made about them? Maybe you're thinking that this person is a slacker. They're unmotivated. Their behavior is unacceptable, and they should probably be let go because they're not adding anything to the team.

And moreover:

What do you *feel*?

If you were working with this person, perhaps you would feel annoyed that others had to cover for them. Maybe you'd feel curious about how an employee could behave this way and still be employed. Maybe there'd be a part of you that wondered what might be going on.

Now what if I told you that the person in this story—the slacker who can't manage to do any of their work—was me?

I was the high performer of the team. I was the one who could do it all, who filled in for everyone else when they needed support.

Until I wasn't.

My watershed moment came when my best friend of more than a decade, Laura, was diagnosed with stage IV brain cancer at the age of twenty-five.

In a flash, I went from being her best friend to being one of her caregivers. I drove her to her doctors' appointments, I helped her pick up her prescriptions, and I was there to keep her company as she faced the reality that she was approaching the end of her life.

All of this was transpiring while I was still working a full-time job as a therapist, seeing thirty or more clients a week, taking on leadership roles, providing learning and development training to the team, and helping to plan the holiday gatherings and celebrations.

Initially, my team was supportive and my leaders checked in with me to see how I was doing. My colleagues held space for my roller coaster of emotions as I navigated the grief of watching my young, beautiful friend die before my eyes.

But eventually, the good graces ended.

After months of depression and struggle, I was told to compartmentalize my grief and focus on work while at work. I was having trouble getting up in the mornings because I was in the depths of a depressive episode, so I was often fifteen to twenty minutes late to work. One day, my supervisor popped up randomly at my work site under the guise of bringing me coffee and wanting to spend time with me, but really, she was there to catch me in the act of being late. This was confirmed when she scheduled a one-on-one with me later that day to discuss my tardiness. She never cared enough to ask me why I was having difficulties showing up on time. She just assumed it was because I was disorganized and not prioritizing my work.

The "work family" that vowed to be there for me withdrew their support, and they started to view me as a distraction. Seemingly overnight, I went from feeling safe and supported to feeling unsafe and isolated. I had never felt more out of sync with my team, and it devastated me. It took me a year in therapy to recover fully from the trauma and feelings of betrayal.

Eventually I left that role to join another agency. Unfortunately, within four weeks of my taking the new job, Laura passed away. I was in the throes of utter devastation, and this workplace responded in a completely different manner from my previous one. I had barely built rapport with my bosses, and my colleagues didn't even know my name, yet they showed up for me in a way that I had never imagined.

When I got the news about Laura and let my office know I would not be coming to work that day, my boss immediately called me. I had accrued zero hours of paid time off (PTO) because I was new, yet she told me to take as much time as I needed to heal. I ended up being in and out of the office for three weeks, and they found a way to forgive the missed time.

I was still having challenges getting up in the mornings because of the depression and grief, so they allowed me to come in after ten a.m. and I just worked a little bit later. Some days, they let me leave early so I could come back the next day refreshed.

Most importantly, they scheduled one-on-one meetings with me, not to talk about the backlog of work or the clients I would be taking on, but instead to see how I was doing. My colleagues made an effort to come by my office and sit with me as tears streamed down my face. They asked me to share about Laura so her legacy could live on.

This is what attunement, or being in tune, looks like in action. It's the small moments that lead to massive outcomes. This experience repaired and healed the hurt from my previous employer, and it restored my faith in what is possible when people have the skills to show up and hold space. This experience, alongside a few others since then, has served as the impetus for my work with corporations, and it is a part of the inspiration for this book.

When I first started speaking about attunement to large corporations like LinkedIn, Godiva, McCain Foods, National Public Radio (NPR), and the Society for Human Resource Management (SHRM), it was my way of applying more than thirteen years of clinical experience as a licensed therapist to my work transforming organizational culture. In the mental health field, we talk about attunement in the context of early childhood relationships and the responsiveness of caregivers to their child's needs. But I realized over the years that attunement matters just as much in adulthood as it does in childhood, and the research supports this assertion.

Looking back, I also realized that speaking and writing on

this topic is actually deeply personal. I worked in a multitude of workplaces that had no idea how to support employees' mental health and well-being, and no clue how to show up and support me when I was struggling emotionally. I knew something needed to change, and that I could be the steward for changing work culture.

I tricked you a bit when I opened this introduction, sharing my story without context. I asked you to identify what you thought and felt from that outsider perspective because our assumptions inform how we move through the world. We form stories based on incomplete information, and it's easy to jump to negative conclusions based on uninformed assumptions. We trust gut reactions, but sometimes they are wrong.

Every day, we see people behaving in ways that bother us, but these behaviors are interpreted out of context.

The colleague who keeps to themselves might get pegged as "not a team player" or "cold," but no one knows they were bullied at previous jobs so they keep to themselves out of self-protection.

The boss who is flaky and frequently reschedules or cancels meetings is juggling work while taking care of a sick child at home as a single parent.

The grocery clerk you label as a jerk because they ignored your "Hello" is struggling to make ends meet with their minimum-wage job and facing eviction.

Your thoughts, feelings, and behaviors are all tied together in a feedback loop, so the negative conclusions you come to as a result of how you feel in the moment can influence the actions you take. Connection, curiosity, and empathy are the remedies. They allow you to paint a clearer picture and decide on a course of action based on a deeper understanding of what's really going on. When you connect with curiosity, you confirm what's actually happening.

As humans, we are relational creatures, wired for connection and belonging. This dates back to the early days of our species, when we relied on one another for survival and lived in close-knit communities. Even though we're no longer being chased by saber-toothed tigers and mastodons, most of us still rely on each other for emotional survival, whether we'd like to admit it or not. It makes sense that this is the case, because feeling connected to those around us bolsters our well-being, contributing to positive outcomes both emotionally and physically. In fact, our relationships are the key to resilience, allowing us to bounce back from adversity and hardship.

Yet we often move through life as ships passing in the night. We are in close proximity, but we never truly connect. What I'm finding is that deep down, most of us desire to feel close to people, but many of us have no idea how to achieve that closeness. Or we've been burned by trying to get close and having it backfire, so we've given up on creating connection.

Our disconnection from one another has contributed to a burgeoning loneliness epidemic that is taking its toll on our emotional, mental, and physical well-being. According to the American Psychiatric Association (APA), in 2024, 30 percent of adults experienced loneliness at least once a week during the past year, and 10 percent said they are lonely every day. Even though we are out of the COVID-19 pandemic and are connecting with friends, family, and colleagues again in real life, 43 percent of adults said that their loneliness has not changed.[1]

This tells me that it's not about whether we are interacting with people or not, because most of us have resumed life as "normal." Instead, it's about the quality of the interactions. And let's be honest—the quality of our daily interactions with others is usually quite poor. If we connect, it's through small talk, platitudes, and surface-level dialogue at work. We leave these encounters feeling hollow and depleted, wishing that there was more to the conversation.

People give us a cursory "How are you?" and we respond with an equally shallow "Fine." If we answer honestly and share with a colleague or a loved one about a struggle we're dealing with or a happy life milestone, it often feels as though they are disinterested in the response. No one wants to feel like they are burdening others with the details of their life, so we all keep to ourselves, walking around with an "I'm okay" mask on.

The feeling of disconnection and disinterest we are experiencing is due to misattunement, or a lack of being in tune with one another. When you tell your boss about the difficulties of coping with depression and they remind you that the expectations and due dates don't change just because you are struggling, that is a moment of misattunement. When you're opening up about a stressful day to a colleague and they're on the phone doomscrolling and not being present for you, that is a moment of misattunement.

Our lives are riddled with moments of misattunement. Missed opportunities for connection that contribute to the widening gulfs between us. Whether it is the sharp tone of voice that someone uses when they are upset with you, the assumption that you're slacking when you make a mistake and miss a deadline at work, or the lack of empathy when you share something personal with your boss, these misattuned moments add up and lead to feelings of discord and disconnection.

When you listen to a symphony as the musicians tune their instruments, it sounds like cacophony. Discordant notes blare out into the audience, and chaotic riffs waft through the air as the clarinet, trombone, violin, and cello all tune simultaneously. Your ears can't parse out one song from another, and it all becomes a jumbled mess. This is the preparation and the individual tuning for the collective creation to come. Eventually, they all tune together to ensure their pitches, tone, and tenor match.

Once the conductor takes the stage and the symphony prepares to perform, the music goes from discordant to harmonious, with each instrument seamlessly blending with the others. This is when the true magic happens. The music that we enjoy is built on the foundation of solid relationships among the musicians playing the notes. They learn to notice the other musicians' breath, timing, crescendos, decrescendos, largo, staccato. They watch one another closely while observing the conductor, taking in all the nonverbal cues and information being disseminated.

This is how attunement functions in work relationships, too. Initially, when you're practicing the skills that I'll be teaching you in this book, you may feel jumbled and mixed up. You'll first learn to become in tune with yourself, which can feel messy and chaotic. But this is normal and expected, because being in tune individually requires you to tolerate some level of discomfort. Doing so means that you build the muscle to manage your own feelings and hold space for others' feelings, too. This is essential for being in tune with others.

You'll notice feelings and body sensations that you may not have noticed before. You'll connect to your inner experience, deepening your self-awareness so you can show up more effectively for yourself and others. Once you've become in tune with yourself, then you start to tune in to other people and what they need. You can hold both your own feelings and needs and theirs without disconnecting from the moment. You start to cultivate the skill set that makes you a master connector in and out of the workplace.

Leaders, middle managers, and team members especially need this skill set because it unlocks the potential for true belonging and connection at work. Leaders (which is a role not based on a title, but rather a mindset) have to lead themselves first before they can effectively lead others. If you don't do your own work, then you will project and play out old dynamics in the way you show up as a leader. It is the single most important journey you can go on.

Without strong leaders creating compassionately connected workplaces, burnout takes hold. Contrary to common belief, isolation and lack of connectivity are two of the major contributors to burnout. In some ways, these feelings are as detrimental as high workload and a lack of resources to get the job done. A work culture that doesn't cultivate a sense of belonging impacts employees' fulfillment and feelings of being supported, which leads to higher rates of attrition, reduced productivity, and diminished outcomes. And the reality is that each employee who leaves due to disconnection and lack of belonging costs an organization, on average, thirty thousand dollars to replace.

Being attuned is not just good for team dynamics and job satisfaction—it's also good for business and the bottom line.

This book is going to take you through the three key elements of attunement: tuning in to yourself, tuning in to others, and learning how to CHECK-IN, which is my step-by-step framework for having more connected conversations at work.

Each chapter includes science-backed strategies and skills that I teach in my corporate speaking, coaching, and consulting engagements, as well as tips for communicating with your neurodivergent peers so you can take into consideration the nuances of these conversations. We cannot use a one-size-fits-all approach, and of course, no group is a monolith, but as someone who is neurodivergent and who has worked with many neurodivergent leaders and teams, I've learned some helpful interventions that may assist you as well.

You'll also read actual client stories (with names and details changed), hear my personal experiences, learn from my cutting-edge research as the first person to examine the impact of attunement on outcomes at work, and explore how the good (and not-so-good) leaders approached interactions, because we learn best through real-world examples.

I am grateful that you are on this journey alongside me, and I know that learning these frameworks will shift your relationships with your leaders and teams. Because we'll be examining your past, present, and future, some tough emotions and experiences may arise. Please take care of yourself, pace yourself, and if need be, reach out to a licensed therapist to assist you beyond what I can do for you in the pages of this book. All I ask of you is to keep an open mind, remain curious, and be willing to push yourself a little outside your comfort zone. Doing so can metamorphose your life. If you're up for the challenge, then let's get started.

Nidhi Tewari, MSW, LCSW

Working Well

Chapter 1

The Science of Attunement

SHE DIDN'T UNDERSTAND what she had done wrong.

Last week, Rachel shared with her boss that she was going to have to step in to take care of her elderly mother. After a recent dementia diagnosis, Rachel's mother's health was rapidly declining, and she could no longer drive to her doctors' appointments. Rachel was now planning how to balance the demands of being both caregiver and employee and figured it was important to loop in her boss about the situation.

Her boss initially responded with an "I'm so sorry to hear that" but then quickly transitioned into "How will this impact your work? Will you be needing tons of time off? What about the projects you're working on? I'm worried you won't be able to handle all this."

The boss technically checked the empathy box, but it wasn't enough. Rachel, whose head was spinning from adjusting to her devastating new reality, was left feeling uncared for. Here she was, courageously informing her boss about this major life change, and all her boss could think about were Rachel's projects and clients.

She had never fallen behind before, so why would that be the first assumption made about her now? Had she given her boss a reason to doubt her capacities? Shouldn't the boss be offering support instead of being so focused on the business?

The two seconds of empathy became overshadowed by the fifteen minutes of work talk.

These scenarios play out in the workplace all the time, and while they are well-intentioned and the boss in this situation may not have felt it was their place to discuss personal issues, the impact is that this response diminishes trust and connection.

In that moment, Rachel learned that her boss was only good for figuring out logistical plans, and she never went back to share life updates with her boss again. Her faith in her boss's ability to show care and consideration disappeared, and it affected her desire to be a part of the team.

This is why attunement and misattunement matter at work.

Attunement, or your ability to be deeply aware of, responsive to, and aligned with the emotional and interpersonal dynamics of colleagues, clients, and the organizational environment, is often spoken about in the context of parent-child dynamics, romantic relationships, or the therapeutic relationship. But for some reason, it's not something we consider or talk about in the work sphere. That's what we're going to change.

The research shows that the relationship between a parent and their child, or lack thereof, significantly impacts the psychological development of that child. We know that we need to be present and be in step with our romantic partner's emotional needs because that's how we show we love and care for them. And the research shows that the single greatest predictor of success in therapy is the therapeutic relationship and how attuned a therapist is to their client's needs.

But we don't talk about the importance of attunement in the workplace, even though interpersonal relationships are make-or-break in this domain. Why is that? Why would work be the exception where attunement doesn't apply? The reality is that companies experience disconnection, attrition, and poorer outcomes because of misattunement. These workplaces need to strengthen the core skills that lead to attunement: flexibility, reading cues, self-regulation, and collaboration.

Our groundbreaking research study on attunement at work found that these four traits, when combined with empathy and compassion, have a tangible and significant impact on outcomes like productivity, job satisfaction, trust, and connection. We'll delve further into the research and these qualities in chapter 5.

Sure, your romantic relationships and parent-child relationships look different from your work relationships. No one expects you to serve as a stand-in parent for a team member or to be the boss-turned-work-therapist helping your teams process their struggles. That's not what I'm talking about here. Leave the therapy work to the trained professionals.

I'm saying that being aware of and responsive to other people's emotions and needs is critical when you're a part of a team or when you're leading people. It's how you create psychological safety and trust within an organization, and it's how you foster a sense of belonging. You don't have to help people heal, but you do need to provide a safe, empathetic space where people can show up and ask for help.

It's the much-needed next evolution of emotional intelligence, or EQ. We used to think that IQ, or your intelligence, cognitive abilities, and critical thinking skills, was most important for success at work. In the last decade, we've learned that your EQ, or ability to understand your and others' emotions, is equally integral to a successful work culture. But the missing pillar to connecting and communicating effectively at work is relational intelligence, or RQ.

EQ is about managing emotions, whereas RQ is about managing relationships.

Relational intelligence is your capacity to help others feel seen and understood by holding your own experience alongside their experience, even when they're disparate realities. It's how you acknowledge missteps and repair relationships when mistakes inevitably happen. Having high RQ means that you're able to adapt to different relational needs and adjust your approach based on personality, culture, and communication style. You recognize the impact of power dynamics in connection and communication, and you navigate these dynamics in a way that enhances safety, trust, and vulnerability.

It's the missing piece in the happy, healthy workplace puzzle.

Attunement is the foundation for strong relational intelligence, but mastering this skill often doesn't come naturally to people. We're usually taught that we should have firm boundaries between our work and personal life, and that the two should never intersect. When life starts getting stressful and it bleeds into your headspace at work, we're told to compartmentalize and focus on the job at hand. Of course, many of you know that this is an unattainable standard that ostracizes anyone who is struggling.

In the old-school management model, leaders are placed high up in the hierarchy, far removed from the people they are leading. They're unaware of the complicated dance between life and work for their team members, with one inevitably affecting the other, and they're not taught how or when to step in to offer support. Many opportunities to accommodate and adapt are missed because of this massive disconnect.

Luckily, the tides are starting to shift. Many corporations are realizing that if they want employees to thrive and stay in their roles, they need more than just pay increases and paid time off. They also need to feel like they are cared for, attended to, and valued as whole people instead of being treated like cogs in the machine.

The COVID-19 pandemic led to much of this shift. For the first time, the world's collective mental health was being impacted by circumstances outside our control. Businesses had to pivot quickly to adapt to the rapidly changing demands, and bosses had to not only learn how to lead remote teams, but also start asking employees about their well-being. Many felt lost and unequipped to support their teams in this way, and it added stress to both leaders and employees alike.

After the "return to normal" in 2022, these well-being initiatives took a back seat because it was assumed that employees were doing okay now. But the lingering effects of the pandemic coupled with the stress of burnout and fatigue from trying to balance so much continues to impact employees' mental health and performance.

Leaders and teams cannot go back to the way the business world operated pre-pandemic, even though that is what still feels familiar. Employees expect more from their workplaces, and rightfully so, given that they're dedicating forty or more hours each week to achieving their companies' revenue goals. The least that employees can receive in return is genuine care and support from their colleagues, managers, and C-suite leaders.

When your employees or team members seek out support or make an appropriate bid for connection from you, but your discomfort gets in the way of being able to show up for them, trust is diminished. That person is less likely to ask for help or share the way their personal life is impacting their work life, which is valuable information that affects the business as well as team dynamics.

Instead, if organizations and leaders can become better attuned to their teams' needs by recognizing the influence that their own life experiences have on how they show up at work, and if they do so by showing interest in employees' lives, by operating from a place of compassion, and by shifting their own biology to connect, then the bottom line is that retention and performance will both improve.

Connection is good for business, period.

Neurodivergent Tip

One of the best shifts to come out of the pandemic years is the flexibility afforded to employees across the globe. Many individuals were permitted to work from home, have flexible work hours, and prioritize their well-being alongside work outcomes. In the last couple of years, we've seen a significant shift back toward return to office (RTO), and that flexibility has diminished.

Caroline worked from home for three years, and she had never felt more productive. She was able to tune out distractions, work in longer blocks of time, and take breaks when she felt she needed to rest. Her hour-long commute, which was previously a source of stress, was eliminated, and this gave her improved focus at work. Instead of buying lunch every day because she didn't get a chance to meal prep, she was able to just go downstairs to her kitchen to eat nutritious food, and she could feel her health improving.

Working from home was a revelation for Caroline. She realized that this is how she was intended to work all along, and it was a game changer for her.

Unfortunately, one day she received an email stating that she was mandated to return to the office five days a week and that she had one month to get herself back to her cubicle.

This evoked immense anxiety for Caroline. She thought, "What if my productivity and focus drop again? What if I feel anxious and can't handle being back in person? I've felt so much better having autonomy and agency over how I work. This is a nightmare."

When she did eventually return, it was so much sensory overload that her fears came true. The sounds of chatter from her colleagues, the constant interruptions from people dropping by her cubicle, and the need to hustle to in-person meetings led to her focus declining. She found it much more difficult to accomplish the same work that she was excelling at before, and she struggled.

Neurodivergent individuals and those with disabilities especially benefit from flexible work options and leaders who are in tune with their needs. Research shows that remote work can provide flexibility in the work environment, affording neurodivergent employees agency over where and how they work, which can positively impact focus and productivity.

It also allows neurodivergent employees to manage sensory sensitivities that are difficult to cope with in an office environment. Many neurodivergent employees struggle with the social expectations of in-person work environments, which can feel overwhelming and distracting, so they may feel safer working from home or in a hybrid arrangement.

This reduces stress for neurodivergent employees, and lower stress = better outcomes.

Finding a job that allows you to work remotely for at least some portion of the week, if that feels better to you as a neurodivergent person, can make a massive difference. I used to see all of my clients in person, but the stressful commute, inability to make lunch at home, and toll of forced social interactions became exhausting for me. Working remotely allows me to set a more reasonable pace to my day, and I enjoy getting to spend my lunch break truly relaxing instead of chatting with people.

Sometimes, work-life balance can be challenging when you work from home, so I have a routine that I use that may be helpful for you, too.

First, I make sure my workspace is separate from my bedroom or other relaxation areas in my home. This way, my brain doesn't associate my bedroom with stress. If you don't have a spot at home, you might go to the library or find a coworking space.

Each day after work, I change out of my work clothes and put them directly in the washer to signal to my brain that the day has transitioned from work to relaxation. Getting into my comfy yoga pants and baggy shirt feels good at the end of a stressful day.

Then, I have a virtual commute, which involves going for a long walk around my neighborhood. The virtual commute takes the place of the stressful, traffic-filled commute, and it helps my brain recognize that my workday is over and I can now disconnect from the stressors of work. It also gives me a chance to process the day, and I get some physical activity as well.

Sync'd Up: The Science of Connection Through Interpersonal Neurobiology

Connection is not just about your emotional experiences. Connection is also a physiologically and neurologically based experience. Your body, including your heart rate, breathing, and demeanor, quite literally sync up to others' bodies when you feel connected. And when you become out of sync, you literally feel it in your mind, body, and heart.

For example, when multiple people watched the same movie separately and their brain activity was measured, they experienced similar fluctuations in brain blood oxygenation, meaning they felt the same emotions at the same time. This synchronization lasted anywhere from seconds to minutes.[1]

What was even more fascinating was that this effect was not just limited to movies. It was observed during conversations, too.[2]

A 2021 research study found that conscious processing can affect heart rate and that audio or audiovisual storytelling, like sharing about a personal experience, leads to each person's heart rate syncing up to another's. This interpersonal synchronization was impacted by attention, which then affected the memory, so being present and focusing were key. The more in sync and in tune the heart rates were, the better the recall of the narrative and the more connected people felt.[3]

You probably know that your mind and body are connected, meaning that when you experience something that evokes anxiety, it creates a physiological response of a racing heart, sweaty palms, and body tension. However, this research shows that not only are your mind and body connected to each other; your mind and body are connected to others' minds and bodies as well.

This is critical information for the workplace because your demeanor and presence when someone is sharing with you impact them, and their demeanor and presence impact you, too.

When someone shares with you that they're feeling down and they're having trouble getting up in the morning to get to work, you have to be cognizant of how you engage. If you listen intently and empathically and respond by saying, "Thanks for trusting me with this. You know, you're not alone, I've had those days, too," then you become in sync and attuned to each other, thereby building trust and connection. This process is known as co-regulation, and it's how one person's nervous system influences another's to help them manage stress and emotions.

When they share that experience with you and you are distracted or uncomfortable so you change the subject, you become out of sync and misattuned. If you become anxious and it's clear that you don't know how to react, the other person will pick up on this and it will lead to misattunement, because they'll fear that they've overshared or burdened you, and they'll start to pull back. They won't come to you again to ask for help because you have shown them that they can't get their needs met by you. They're looking to you moment to moment to see whether you're in step or not, and each time you're not attuned is a deterioration of psychological safety. Even something small like immediately changing the subject back to a work topic can cause these ruptures to happen.

The opposite holds true, too. Micromoments of connection, like remembering that your colleague loves concerts and asking them about seeing their favorite artist over the weekend, or circling back to check in on a team member whose sister is going through cancer treatments, are examples of attunement. It's not the grand gestures—it's the smaller, consistent actions that foster trust and connection.

One way to dive a bit deeper into this idea is through the field of research for a concept called interpersonal neurobiology.

Interpersonal neurobiology was coined by psychiatrist Dr. Daniel Siegel as a way to understand the overlap between the mind, the brain, and our relationships. He utilizes neuroscience, attachment theory, and psychology to better understand the way people engage interpersonally and how these experiences shape the development and functioning of the brain. The way the brain functions and develops in turn impacts emotional, social, and cognitive processes.[4]

The goal, according to Dr. Siegel, is to strengthen our integration, or the cohesion between different parts of the brain, and to develop our mindsight, or the perception of your mind and others' minds. Being able to learn the skills to enhance both of these areas allows you to show up from a place of empathy and compassion for other people, including your colleagues and team members.

Mindsight encourages you to become introspective about your internal experience. It helps you break patterns of behavior that repeatedly get in the way of connecting, so you can respond in a way that considers your needs alongside others'.

For example, when someone shares feedback at work that feels critical or unexpected, you might respond in a way that is defensive and that tries to invalidate the other person's opinions. You might just write it off or feel angry that they would say such a thing. This happens because the feedback feels like an attack on your efforts or a mischaracterization of your potential, so you react in a strong manner that creates disconnection. Your boss's need is for their feedback to be heard, but your need is to receive validation alongside the feedback.

Mindsight teaches you to observe and name the experience so you can better understand it, which in turn allows you to show up differently in the interaction. You can focus on the emotion, see what's inside, accept it, let it go, and transform it in that process of release.[5] Telling yourself, "That was uncomfortable. When I got that feedback, I felt attacked," will help you to handle it differently in the future.

Dr. Siegel's research found that engaging in the mindsight process actually changes the structures of the brain. What you focus on and how you focus on it shape your brain's physiology, which means you are enacting change on a neurobiological level. These new connections in your brain, also known as neuroplasticity, don't just happen in childhood—they also happen in adulthood, reinforcing the hope that it's never too late to cultivate these skills and change.[6]

Attached: How You Connected to People Earlier in Life Determines Your Relationships Now

Think back to your earliest memories growing up. Maybe you remember once when you were playing outside, fell off the swing set, and scraped your knee. You probably ran inside crying because you were hurt. Who was there to comfort you? Who was there to soothe you in your moment of distress?

These early moments are part of attachment, or the emotional bond between an infant and its parent figure. I'm sure you're wondering what this has to do with work. Well, for better or for worse, your early attachments from childhood and adolescence shape the way you engage with people interpersonally as an adult.

Some of you had attachment figures who were consistent, stable, and loving. When you scraped your knee, they hugged you, put a bandage on the scrape, and sat with you until you felt better. This is secure attachment. You learned that your caregiver was a consistent, safe base to return to during good times and bad.

Some of you had attachment figures who got upset and felt distressed by your tears, so they yelled at you to stop crying or they minimized your pain and told you to toughen up. You learned to suppress and disconnect from your feelings because emotions equaled weakness. You might have felt anxious, and didn't want them to be mad or for you to be perceived as weak, so you went to your room to finish crying by yourself. This is insecure attachment. You didn't have a caregiver who was there to comfort you and teach you how to cope with your emotions.

Some of you had caregivers who were there to dry your tears sometimes, but at other times, their patience had run out and they ignored you or got upset with you. The consistency was lacking, and you were constantly left wondering which parental personality you'd be having to navigate in that moment. This is disorganized attachment. You didn't know what to expect, so sometimes you felt anxious, sometimes you felt withdrawn, and sometimes you felt supported.

These early interactions taught you a lot about the world around you. They taught you which reactions were tolerable and which were deemed unacceptable. They taught you who was safe to turn to when you were in pain or struggling and who you needed to avoid. These messages show up subconsciously in how you tolerate pain and discomfort now, which influences how you hold space for other people as well. It takes work and insight to move through the knee-jerk reactions that developed earlier in your life so you can tolerate other people's emotions.

In my years of working as a therapist, I've found that attachment doesn't just stop in infancy. You likely had other attachment figures, like coaches, teachers, mentors, and friends, who taught you lessons about what was safe versus unsafe. These relationships also have a significant impact on your interpersonal relationships in adulthood. If you were bullied and picked on in middle school or high school, then chances are you moved through the world feeling like people are not trustworthy or kind. These thoughts become your core beliefs, and they shape how you interpret the world around you.

Attachments continue to form in adulthood to romantic partners, friends, and, yes, colleagues and bosses. When these relationships are healthy and go well, they show you that relationships are safe and trusting. But when these relationships are unhealthy and disintegrate, they reinforce the perception that relationships aren't safe and people aren't trustworthy.

For example, I had a client, let's call him Sam, who worked in a large corporation. He had grown attached to and become friends with a work colleague, Chris. For years, they ate lunch together, took on projects together, and even went to happy hours after work to catch up. Then one day, Chris suddenly turned on Sam when he saw that Sam was outshining him. Chris started sharing information that Sam had disclosed in confidence and gave him the cold shoulder, which disrupted Sam's sense of safety and belonging.

Sam carried this experience with him for years, and he had a difficult time trusting his colleagues no matter which job he took. He feared that they would try to sabotage him if he got close to them and started to excel. Being successful evoked anxiety for him, and it took him time in therapy to get to a place where he could put himself out there again for promotions and special projects.

It wasn't until five years later, when Sam met Judy, that he felt he could trust in his colleagues again. Judy was smart and, most importantly, secure in herself, so when Sam shined at work, Judy celebrated him. Judy made it a point to be a woman of her word, so when she said that she would keep something between them, she meant it. They edified one another, and Judy showed Sam that not everyone is hypercompetitive or out to sabotage.

Your adult relationships can heal attachment wounds. Healthy relationships can undo the damage of unhealthy ones. That idea of neuroplasticity applies here, too.

This is part of why it's critical to ensure every workplace is psychologically safe and attuned. People can't do their best work or show up as their best selves when they have the fears and stressors from previous workplaces being reinforced in their current jobs. Be the one to break the cycle by learning to be in tune with yourself and with others.

Instantaneous Instincts: Fight, Flight, Freeze, and Fawn at Work

Working in toxic environments and dealing with unhealthy work dynamics put you in survival mode. You're just trying to make it through each day without incident, and it takes immense amounts of energy to navigate it all. When your brain enters survival mode, you'll react in one of four ways: fight, flight, freeze, or fawn.

These responses are designed to give you the best chance of survival in a life-or-death situation, but they can get activated when high-stress moments occur at work as well.

If you have a boss who intentionally leaves you off email chains or consistently shares incomplete information with you so you can't get the job done, you might experience hypervigilance, or an elevated state of constantly assessing threats around you. You don't know who or what to trust, and you feel the need to be on guard, looking out for any signs of danger.

If a colleague then accidentally forgets to CC you on an email one time, you will likely jump to the conclusion that they're trying to sabotage you, just like your boss is doing. You might feel like the entire workplace is against you, even though there isn't evidence to back up that assertion. As a result, you might point a finger at your colleague and confront them about their behavior, explaining to them that you see right through their tactics.

This type of reaction is called a fight response. A fight response at work looks like defensiveness, blaming, and accusing behavior. It's a way for you to stand your ground and stay safe in what is perceived to be a moment of danger. This is not a desired response at work, because although it's natural to feel discontent or frustration, we have to express our emotions and needs in a way that is respectful of others. We can be direct and clear without being rude or aggressive. We have to learn ways to shift out of the fight response into a more regulated state. If a team member reacts in a way that seems disproportionate to the situation, leaders and coworkers can clarify intentions and try to better understand why the person is reacting so strongly, which reestablishes safety and reduces the feeling of being targeted.

I once worked with a corporate client, let's call him Jeremy, who would get overwhelmed when too many tasks were assigned to him. Jeremy's boss would give him two or three projects at a time, and Jeremy would also be in charge of learning and development initiatives within his team, so he started to feel his stress levels rising. Everyone else was swamped, so he couldn't ask for help, but he didn't see any way to accomplish all these tasks.

Instead of telling his boss about his challenges and asking for a reprieve, Jeremy started avoiding all emails related to one of the projects. He felt like he was out of his depth with the project because it required data analytics, which was not Jeremy's strong suit, so he just tried to focus on everything else outside of that assignment.

His avoidance got so bad that his boss had to schedule a one-on-one to address his behavior. Jeremy's lack of responsiveness was getting in the way of the client receiving their deliverables. Finally, Jeremy let his boss know that when he felt overwhelmed, he tended to try to escape the situation instead of asking for help. He didn't know where to begin with that project, so he just didn't start.

This information was critical for Jeremy's boss to hear, because now they could ensure that they conducted more check-ins and looked at how Jeremy's projects were going long before they were due.

Jeremy's avoidance and escapism are typical of a flight response at work. People who experience a flight response might avoid the situation to the point of resignation, even if they are an otherwise high-performing employee. Employees who flee would rather leave the situation than face it head-on because dealing with it feels incredibly overwhelming. Leaders can reduce this overwhelm by offering support and problem-solving the issues that are preventing the work from getting done. For example, you could talk through the steps needed to complete the task so overwhelm is reduced and discuss any elements of the tasks that still feel daunting. Often, just walking through the process and clarifying what's needed helps people get rolling.

Another corporate client, let's call them Connor, often felt disconnected when they experienced too much stress at work. Normally, Connor was an active participant in team meetings, and they were usually willing to step in to support colleagues who were struggling emotionally. But something shifted after Connor was promoted to a management position.

Their team members came to them, asking for guidance on which tasks to prioritize, and Connor had a hard time giving a concrete response. They would always say they didn't know and they needed time to make a decision, but even after a few days, their team still didn't have an answer. This created confusion and frustration for the team, who had previously known Connor to be decisive and supportive as a team member.

Connor continued to seem withdrawn and indecisive, and finally one day their leader checked in on them. It turned out that Connor was feeling overwhelmed in their new managerial role, and their response was to freeze. They would struggle with decision-making, they would retreat to their office away from others, and they would feel disconnected from themselves and their team.

Their boss was able to talk through the different areas

contributing to overwhelm, and Connor started feeling more grounded. They got permission to ask their boss for feedback when they felt stuck so they could get themselves out of this frozen state and know that they had support to work through their problems.

A freeze state causes a shutdown response, and reorientation to the present, alongside connection and support, can help shift out of this type of dissociated reaction. Leaders can keep this in mind when they see changes in demeanor that might be indicative of a freeze response.

Finally, I provided therapy to a client I'll call Teresa, whose job was in the corporate sphere. Teresa was always unbelievably helpful and consistently raised her hand to take on new tasks at work. She would often continue working after five p.m., and she made it a point to never leave tasks undone. She planned all the company holiday gatherings, mentored others on the team, and carried more work than anyone else.

Over a few months, Teresa started to experience the classic symptoms of burnout. She tried to rest on the weekends, but she always felt exhausted, no matter how much downtime she had. She was losing passion for her work, and she wasn't feeling fulfilled in her role any longer. The stress levels got so high that she became ill and ended up taking off three weeks from work to recuperate.

When Teresa returned to work, her boss checked in to see how she was doing, and Teresa was afraid to acknowledge she was stressed. She worried that her boss would see her as less capable or competent, and she didn't want to get in trouble for feeling overwhelmed. Teresa's boss referred her to the Employee Assistance Program, which is a suite of benefits that often includes access to a therapist for free, financial planning, and other services. A few weeks later, Teresa scheduled a one-on-one with her boss to discuss what had happened as she explored her patterns with me through her Employee Assistance Program.

It turned out that Teresa had experienced a fawn response, in which she didn't feel safe saying no or setting boundaries. People who fawn have learned to abandon their own needs to take care of others because that's how they have received connection in the past. Teresa was so scared that her boss wouldn't trust her anymore if she was honest about her overwhelm that she pushed past all the signs of burnout to please her boss.

People pleasers like Teresa need leaders who will remind them that they are allowed to set limits and say no. They may struggle with limit setting, so leaders can step in and pass off responsibilities to others in order to protect the people pleaser's energy. The trickiest part about leading people pleasers is that others benefit from their overfunctioning, but the people pleasers run the risk of burning out and quitting if they don't receive the support they need.

Neurodivergent Tip

As a therapist who is diagnosed with both generalized anxiety disorder and attention deficit hyperactivity disorder (ADHD), I can tell you that my conditions impact the way I perceive information. I've always been a people pleaser who wants to do the best work possible, and although I hate to admit it, I crave validation and affirmation from others. I'm working on relying on this less, but it's a part of how I know I'm on the right track and I'm doing a good job. After I give a talk to a corporation or an event, I anxiously await the feedback to see how everything landed.

A few years ago, I worked for government agencies as an outpatient therapist. One day, after I turned in some work that needed my boss's feedback, I received an email from her asking, "Can we talk?" She sent me a calendar invite shortly after. When I saw that email and the invite, I instantly went into an anxiety spiral. My heart began pounding, my palms started dripping with sweat, and my thoughts raced like Usain Bolt at the Olympics.

There was no context and no information to let me know what this conversation would be about. Was she going to fire me? Did she hate the work I was submitting? Did I miss a deadline so now I was getting reprimanded? The possibilities of all the awful scenarios were endless. I reluctantly responded, letting my boss know I was free later that day to meet. Even though I wanted to avoid the interaction, I knew my anxiety would keep me up at night if I didn't get to the bottom of this.

At 3:30 p.m. that afternoon, I took some deep breaths before I entered my boss's office, ready to get reamed. She sat down across from me in those bluish-gray cloth government chairs, and I braced myself with clenched fists. "Stay cool, stay calm," I told myself.

After a couple minutes of small talk, she looked at me and said, "I just wanted to meet to talk about the great work you're doing and to see about putting together some additional groups for the summer. What are some topics you think would be good?"

My internal monologue went wild with all the things I wished I could say to her. I thought to myself, "WHAT?! You wanted to meet for this?? This could have been an email. Do you have any idea how much I've agonized all day over this meeting? How inconsiderate."

When someone has anxiety and they do not have adequate information, their brain will fill in the gaps with worst-case scenarios. All of my anxiety could have been prevented had she just provided some additional clues about the purpose of the meeting and what was going to be discussed. Had she done this, she could have saved me from having the three mini panic attacks I experienced throughout the day.

Simple fixes can include providing context and saying, "Can we chat later today about the project we're collaborating on together? I would love to brainstorm ideas with you." This gives anxious people the opportunity to mentally prepare for the conversation to come. It also alleviates any stress and anxiety that come from the stories we use to fill in the lack of information. Remember this key communication tenet when communicating with people who are neurodivergent: Clear is kind.

If you're the person on the receiving end of this type of email, it's easy to jump to the worst-case scenario and think it automatically spells doom. While it's initially easier said than done, it's critical that you practice grounding yourself in the facts. The reality is that many people are unaware of how they come across when they send emails and calendar invites like this. They're so focused on being efficient in their communications that they forget about the importance of considering how their message will be received.

Thinking of other explanations for someone's behavior stops you from personalizing what's going on. The psychology concept of the spotlight effect explains how we often feel that others are focused on us, but usually people are in their own worlds, thinking about themselves.

Until you have more context and information, you could say to yourself, "This feels scary because there is so much that is unknown, but that doesn't mean this is a sign that I'm in trouble or getting laid off. It might be that my boss was in a rush when sending the email, and it's something totally innocuous, like wanting to talk about a project or following up on a previous conversation. I'll pause on trying to fortune-tell what's coming until I have more information."

Stop the anxiety spiral, and notice the alternative possibilities.

Part I

Tuning In to Yourself

You're probably wondering why a business book has a personal development section. Well, believe it or not, your work relationships bring up all the same reactions and stress that you experience in your personal relationships. It's all interconnected.

When you think about bettering your work relationships, you're likely thinking about understanding and connecting with the other person. But before you're able to effectively build stronger relationships with your team and colleagues, you have to develop a deeper relationship with your own inner world.

Self-awareness precedes interpersonal awareness.

In this chapter, you'll learn how to lead yourself so you can then lead in your work interactions. You'll start connecting the dots between your own life experiences and the ways that you show up in the workplace, and you'll learn how to move from reacting to responding.

You have to do the internal work in order to see the external results.

Chapter 2

Mirrors and Models: Reflecting on Your Childhood Relationships

I FELL TO the ground in devastation, tears streaming down my face.

I was in third grade, and I loved school with all my heart. It felt like my safe haven and a place where I could truly be myself. But this morning was different. This morning, I received a piece of heartbreaking news right before hopping on the bus.

As a first-generation Indian American, I was never in close proximity to my grandparents. They lived in India and were too old to travel frequently to the States, and while I had heard hundreds of stories about them, I had spent only a few months with them.

But those few months were some of my fondest memories. I remember when my grandfather, better known as my Dadaji, visited me in the States and showered me with so much love. We used to walk to the playground down the street every day, and he would push me on the swings, higher and higher.

At bedtime, he would sit with my sister and me and read us books in Hindi about the great kings of India, like Birbal and Akbar. Dadaji was a quiet man, so these moments of connection meant the world to me. He was one of my few links to my family's culture.

That morning in third grade, my parents gave me the news that my Dadaji had passed away from stage IV pancreatic cancer. Being so young, I had a limited grasp on what cancer was or the finality of death, but based on my dad's solemn expression, my gut told me that Dadaji wouldn't be coming back.

At the time, I couldn't understand why I was sent off to school like it was a normal day. Looking back now with adult eyes, I'm sure my family had to buy tickets to go to India and make preparations for Dadaji's cremation, which is led by the oldest brother, my dad. But in that moment, it felt like I had to keep all these big feelings inside.

I held it together on the bus, fiddling with the keychain I had dangling off of my JanSport backpack. I didn't have words for what I was feeling at the time, but I think I was numb and in shock.

I managed to make it into my first class and put my backpack into my little cubby with my name tag above the hook. I grabbed my pencil case and started walking over to my desk to begin history class, and suddenly I was overcome with emotion.

I fell to my knees and started sobbing. My poor little heart was shattered in a million pieces as I felt grief and loss for the first time in my life. Everyone turned to look at me. I could feel their alarm and unease. It was out of character for me to be crying like this.

To my surprise, my teacher, Mrs. Shapiro, rushed over to

me, got down on her knees, and started asking me in a pleading tone, “What’s wrong, Nidhi? Are you okay? Oh honey, what’s going on?” Bleary-eyed and gasping for air between cries, I squeaked out, “My grandfather died.”

Mrs. Shapiro scooped me up in her arms and gave me a big squeeze. She looked so concerned and reacted so compassionately. As she directed the rest of the class to start working on the Native American history unit, she whisked me away, holding my hand as we walked toward the school counselor’s office.

She looked at me and said, “I’m so sorry, Nidhi. I can tell you loved your grandfather very much, and I know this is so hard.” I couldn’t say much at the time, but this simple act of empathy and validation made me feel less alone in my grief.

Eventually, I was sent home and got to be with my family during this tough time. My parents talked to me about what my Dadaji’s death meant, and they helped me see that we would get through this together. I could feel their support as I tried to find meaning after this loss. When I finally returned to school later that week, Mrs. Shapiro pulled me aside to check on me again. Her genuine care and concern have stuck with me.

She became one of my first models of how to show empathy and compassion to others going through a difficult time.

Of course I didn’t have the language then, but now I know that Mrs. Shapiro gave me an attuned response. She saw this little kid having big emotions, and she literally got on my level when she kneeled in front of me and talked to me. She didn’t try to tell me to push through or get upset that I was disrupting the class by having her escort me to the office. She gave me what I needed, which was kindness, understanding, and the feeling that I wasn’t alone.

Such early experiences of attunement shape the way you support others and the way you expect to be supported. When you experience care and consideration in difficult moments, you learn how to provide that same care to others, and you expect to receive that same care in return. If you're left to figure out your feelings on your own, it can be difficult to know how to support yourself, let alone others, since it was never modeled for you.

I see this all the time with the leaders I coach. Many grew up in cultures, family systems, and communities where emotions were ignored or, worse, viewed as a weakness. They never learned how to sit with their emotions, express their emotions, or support others' emotions. When they're promoted into a leadership role and are leading a team, they're expected to provide emotionally and relationally intelligent responses. Instead of knowing what to say or do, they clam up and avoid or dismiss the feelings.

This of course impacts the trust and safety the team feels, and before they know it, no one is coming to them to ask for help because they can't trust that they'll receive a supportive response.

The good news is that the healthy, emotionally attuned relationships you have later in life can make up for a lack of them earlier in life. Having friends, coaches, leaders, therapists, teachers, and others who show you what it means to be emotionally in tune can bridge those knowledge gaps.

Although I grew up in a culture in which emotions and mental health were rarely, if ever, discussed, I had teachers who showed me how to be emotionally attuned.

I had many models like Mrs. Shapiro when I was a child. Most were teachers who recognized my individual gifts, interests, and strengths, and they showed that they were attuned by investing energy in developing my skills in those areas. They also helped me get through some of the toughest times of my life, including a period when I lost the ability to walk in high school. I was wheelchair bound and in a dark place emotionally, missing tons of school as I underwent a litany of MRIs and CT scans to figure out what was wrong, and the majority of my teachers were not only accommodating in terms of adjusting my school workload, they were emotionally supportive as well. They checked on me, they helped me feel less alone, and when kids picked on me for being in a wheelchair, they stepped in to protect me.

I clung to movies like *Matilda,* the story of a smart, young girl who is born into the wrong family. Her unemotional parents and brother don't get how special she is, and Ms. Honey, Matilda's sweet-as-pie teacher, protects her and, ultimately, adopts her. Ms. Honey became my ideal for how adults should act. TV shows like *The Fresh Prince of Bel-Air* and *Full House* modeled good conflict resolution and repairing relationships in a loving way. They became a template for the family I'd want to have one day when I became a grown-up.

Even though these movies and shows were glamorized, Disney-fied versions of reality, they still taught people something important. You can go through hard things, talk about the hard things, and come out the other side stronger and closer.

Why do these stories and people matter? *Because we often model and mirror how others treat us and how we see others are being treated.* Their behaviors become our templates for how we navigate the world.

If we didn't have anyone in our lives to show us how to hold space for emotions or sit with the hard stuff, then we face an uphill battle in learning how to do these things as adults. Any emotions outside the happiness spectrum get labeled as bad, and we'll do anything in our power to disconnect from them because they evoke discomfort.

We'd rather drink, eat, or spend away the uncomfortable feelings, repressing them or projecting them onto everyone else around us.

It's not just our childhood relationships with adults that influence how we move through the world. Our friendships growing up also teach us about interpersonal dynamics.

If you were bullied and picked on by your school peers, then you likely developed the belief that you can't trust people or that relationships are unsafe. You might have also come to believe that you are not good enough or not deserving of love.

Whether or not you were able to speak up and were believed when you did report these early-in-life incidents often influences whether you'll report workplace transgressions in adulthood. If your childhood experiences were denied and the bully escalated because you tried to address the issue, then you're less likely to report similar issues today. Why would you expose yourself to the compounded trauma of the bullying *and* not being believed?

On the other hand, if a friend stood up and defended you, then that might have mitigated some of your feelings of being alone and completely misunderstood. You might be more inclined to trust a vetted colleague when you're being targeted at work if you had a good experience before.

These experiences become the road map for how we navigate similar situations in the future.

When I was picked on in school for being "too much"—too loud, too smart, too outgoing, too fill-in-the-blank—it made me self-conscious about how I showed up in all facets of my life. When I tried to speak to trusted adults about it, it was never addressed and I felt like I wasn't believed.

I carried that narrative that I was "too much" with me into the workplace, and for a long time, I had challenges speaking up, saying no, or being the one with good ideas. I worried anything would place a target on my back, so I shrunk myself.

Reflecting on it now, I can see that the lack of attunement and support I experienced in childhood was rearing its head in my adult life at work. The past was clearly becoming present.

Many of you have likely experienced being bullied or excluded in the workplace, when your team reacts to your presence in a way that leads you to feel as though you need to edit and shape yourself in order to fit into the mold. They make it seem like it's about you being a culture fit, but in reality, they're uncomfortable with the energy you bring to the table.

I also wondered if the bullying I experienced was all in my head, or if there was something wrong with me, because no one in a position of power would acknowledge that what was happening was wrong.

This is a common thread with many of the leaders I've worked with in therapy. They wondered if they were overreacting or just reading too much into the situation. Perhaps it was all a big misunderstanding, and the situation wasn't as awful as it felt in the moment.

But as they unpacked their work experiences with me in session, the picture came into focus: They were being targeted and gaslit by others.

They told me that lots of colleagues saw what was happening and even called it out, so they mustered up the courage and shared their concerns with their bosses. To their dismay, they were told they were misunderstanding the other person, even though they had witnesses who heard what was said. This was classic gaslighting, or psychological manipulation intended to call into question their sanity and reasoning abilities.

They internalized this feedback and started gaslighting themselves. If their boss said it was a misunderstanding, then there must not be anything else to it, right? Wrong. Even the presence of witnesses corroborating their experiences wasn't enough to convince them that they were mistreated. They continued to question their reality and downplay the hardship.

Through my work with these leaders, I found that many of them had experienced this type of gaslighting in the past.

They had parents who made mean-spirited comments but then told them that they were being too sensitive. They were once bouncy, effervescent children who were told that they were annoying or overactive, so they started to dull their shine. Some of them had coaches who would relentlessly criticize them under the guise of toughening them up. Their work experiences reinforced those earlier models of harmful interpersonal relationships, and similar narratives from the past arose. They thought, "Maybe there's something wrong with me. Maybe it's all in my head. Maybe I am too much or not good enough."

No wonder the go-to reaction was to question their reality. Their childhood experiences were full of people questioning and minimizing their feelings.

They learned that in order to survive, they needed to just suck it up. They learned to abandon their own needs to keep the peace. Just like they stopped sharing with adults when they were younger, they never went to their bosses with concerns again, and they stopped trusting their team.

The research explains why this happens. How a leader responds to whistleblowing and employee concerns can impact whether or not the employee opens up in the future.

One study found that offering protections to those who may blow the whistle is critical for people to feel safe to speak up again.[1] Another study highlights the importance of ensuring there are policies and practices in place to protect individuals. These protections and action steps encourage employees to open up again, but a lack of protection and belief dissuades future whistleblowing, allowing a toxic, unethical culture to persist.[2]

This is part of why so many unhealthy cultures struggle to change. A culture is defined by the behaviors it's willing to tolerate. When leaders show that they're willing to turn a blind eye to bullying and mistreatment, they teach employees that it's pointless to speak up. Toxicity continues to fester, and people decide to leave because that's where they have control.

Think back on your own life experiences, and reflect on what was modeled for you and what you mirrored behaviorally as a result.

Which relationships were healthy and modeled empathy, compassion, and emotional attunement?

Which experiences taught you that the world is unsafe, that you shouldn't trust people, and that you are unworthy?

We've all had both ends of the spectrum, and those experiences become the lenses through which we view the world.

It's amazing to see how, for better or worse, we are all kids in adult bodies and clothing. That awareness becomes the foundation for healing, and it opens up the opportunity for you to start showing up differently in the here and now.

Neurodivergent Tip

Unfortunately, many neurodivergent individuals did not have strong models to help them navigate bullying earlier in life. Their parents told them to ignore the bullies or tell the teacher, which often backfired and allowed the bullying to continue. These models for how to handle mistreatment impacted the way they now engage at work.

Destiny was diagnosed with autism at a young age, and she struggled to make friends at school. She would go down a conversational rabbit hole on her special interests, like dinosaurs or ancient Egypt, and her peers found her to be "weird" and "boring." They would poke fun at her and exclude her from birthday parties and group activities, and she often felt like she was not accepted by her peers.

When she would come home after school in tears because of the constant mistreatment, her parents would tell her that she should just ignore her classmates' behavior and that she needed to be the bigger person instead of standing up for herself, which led to her becoming passive. She started isolating herself, and she dreaded going to school because it was painful being persistently rejected.

As an adult, Destiny continued to approach bullying in the workplace using the model she was given in childhood. She tried to be the bigger person and just let it go, but the bullying continued to escalate. She didn't have the right skills to know how to address the behavior with her colleagues, and she didn't feel comfortable going to her boss because she thought she might be viewed as weak.

Instead, she endured the bullying until she couldn't take it anymore and withdrew from the team. Just like in her school days, Destiny felt like she needed to leave in order to protect herself.

She needed her boss and colleagues to step up and intervene when they saw the bullying occur, but they didn't.

This scenario often plays out in the workplace, and the solution is to have a speak-up culture. Addressing unhealthy dynamics needs to be normalized and rewarded, and people need to feel safe going to leadership about issues like bullying. Colleagues can help create a speak-up culture by courageously intervening when they see negative behaviors occur.

For example, if a team member interrupts and bulldozes over another team member, you can pause and say, "I think that [team member] was mid-thought and hadn't finished sharing. Let's hear the rest of what he has to say, and then I'd love to hear your insights."

These micro-interventions matter and need to become more common in the workplace. Having a speak-up culture preserves psychological safety and connection, which ultimately impacts other outcomes as well.

For many neurodivergent employees and leaders, leaving a job when no one addresses the bullying at work is the only way to ensure your mental health stays intact. Your loyalty needs to have limits, and your well-being has to be a priority.

When bosses and colleagues allow mistreatment to occur, it's a signal that they don't prioritize psychological safety in the workplace. Sometimes, the bully is also the high performer, and bosses would rather passively allow their behavior to continue than risk losing someone who has high output.

Continuing to speak up can increase the likelihood of being targeted or being viewed as the problem, so the best option at that point is to take your talents elsewhere.

Past Problems, Present Perceptions: Recognizing the Past-Present Connection

Steven put down his coffee on his desk and silenced his phone before taking a deep breath. He sat tensely in his swivel chair and stretched his back, preparing himself for the conversation to come. His anxiety was at a ten because today was the day he had to talk with Julie about letting her go. Although Steven had made it through other tough conversations, he had never had to fire someone before.

As the boss, Steven tried to have multiple coaching conversations about Julie's performance issues and her lack of consistency at work. He asked all the right questions to diagnose what was going on and provided the appropriate feedback to improve the outcomes, but Julie didn't seem to apply the advice. Steven knew what he had to do, but he was dreading it.

Julie showed up ten minutes late for the meeting and seemed unconcerned by her tardiness. No apologies or acknowledgment. She took a seat and jumped right into small talk. "How's your week going so far? It's hard to believe it's a new year already, it feels like time just flew by," she said.

"Yeah, it's really wild," Steven replied, trying to hide his annoyance and wanting to go ahead and get this over with. He started hesitantly, trying to find his footing in this conversation.

"So, Julie, we've had a few conversations over the past year about some challenges with your performance. You were late getting back to clients a number of times, you missed project deadlines three times, and you've had issues with tardiness. I know that we discussed some ways to organize your time differently so you don't miss important priorities, but we haven't seen the improvement we need..."

Before Steven could land the plane and tell Julie that she would no longer be employed with their organization, Julie interrupted with a bit of an attitude.

"Well, I've had a lot going on, and I'm doing my best. I tried using your techniques, but they just weren't working for me. New priorities kept popping up, and I didn't know what to focus on. I'm doing my best."

Steven felt thrown off. He hadn't anticipated being cut off

and then having to recover his composure. He had rehearsed lots of scenarios, but an aggressive interaction was not one of them.

Steven picked back up. "I definitely appreciate your efforts and understand that life has thrown a lot your way. It sounds like it's been a tough year. However, because these issues have persisted over the past year and these difficulties weren't communicated over the course of this year, unfortunately, we're going to have to terminate your employment, effective immediately."

The silence was deafening. Julie just sat there, scowling silently at Steven. No response, just a stare. Steven could feel his anxiety rising. His heart started racing, his palms got sweaty, and he shifted in his chair to discharge some of his nervous energy. Julie wasn't going to break the silence, so Steven had to chime in.

"I know this is a lot to process, but the decision is final."

Julie responded angrily, "I can't believe this. You're firing me? After I gave so much to this team for the past year? I just think this is so messed up, especially when there are other slackers on the team. What am I supposed to do now? The job market is so hard out there. You know I have a family to care for. You're heartless."

Before he could respond, Julie left the room and started packing her personal items in a box.

After contacting HR to get through the final steps of releasing Julie, Steven retreated to his car, went for a drive to a Walmart parking lot, and got really angry.

He knew this conversation hadn't gone the way he'd hoped, but he couldn't figure out why he was reacting so strongly. He normally did well under pressure, but he was crumbling. Of course, he'd expected Julie to be upset—that's a normal reaction. But there was something that hit a bit differently this time. He brought the situation to his next executive coaching session with me, and we examined what had happened together.

What Steven didn't realize at the time is that the past becomes present, and as a mentor once told me, if your reaction is hysterical, its roots are historical.

The memory networks that are formed earlier in life link up with present-day experiences, so when a situation looks like, sounds like, and feels like a past situation, we react similarly. These neural pathways get reinforced, and the likelihood of that conditioned reaction increases until new, more adaptive ways of reacting are created.

A compilation of leadership research published in 2023 by Sokol Loci and Judita Peterlin underscores how life stories influence a leader's identity, core values, and meaning-making system. These past experiences justify behaviors in the present, and a leader's difficult family circumstances, high parental expectations, and past experiences in leadership roles since childhood affect both how they perceive information obtained and how they use that information in future events.[3]

In essence, the life experiences you've had at earlier points in your development provide a framework for how you respond now as a leader. These schemas form the foundation for future interactions, and they subconsciously drive the bus.

For example, if you grew up in a household with high parental expectations and where perfection was the goal, then you might have difficulties making mistakes and acknowledging missteps. You likely feel the pressure to have all the answers and to get it right every time.

You might have been shamed or felt inadequate when you messed up, so now you shame spiral and beat yourself up whenever something doesn't go according to plan. You may have core beliefs like "I should have known better," "I have to be perfect," or "I'm incompetent." You're probably less likely to seek support when you need it because you've learned that you need to figure it all out on your own.

Once you unpack the impact of these unreasonable parental expectations, you'll start to see that perfection is unattainable and that mistakes are inevitable. In fact, failure is the birthplace of success. You'll stop placing immense pressure on yourself, and in turn, this will improve the expectations that you set for the people you're leading.

Returning to Steven's dilemma: As I spoke with him about his strong reaction to his conversation with Julie, Steven began reflecting on his childhood.

We realized that conflict had always been hard for him.

Growing up, he never felt like he could speak up without it causing a blowup. Whenever he had to tell his parents no or didn't agree with their demands, he was met with anger and resentment.

He recalled an argument with his mother. When she was younger, Steven's mother played the violin in the symphony orchestra, and she forced Steven to take music classes. Steven tried the classes for a couple years to appease his mother, but he secretly hated going each week. He tried hinting at how he disliked the classes and even said a few times that he didn't enjoy playing violin, but his mother insisted that with time, he would fall in love with orchestra. He was really talented and ranked as the first chair in his school, but his heart just wasn't in it.

When Steven was twelve, his mother told him she was going to enroll him in a performing arts school so he could focus on music. Steven was never consulted, and the decision was made for him. All of a sudden, he was expected to pick up and start fresh at a new school without having any say.

Feeling frustrated with his mother, Steven said, "What?! Mom, I told you before, music is not my thing. I hate going to orchestra rehearsals, and the performances suck the life out of me. I don't want to go to a performing arts school, and all my friends are at the school I'm in. I'll have to start over, and I don't want that."

Steven's mom angrily replied, "Do you know how hard I had to work to get you into this school? You're so ungrateful. I can't believe you're acting this way. You're a spoiled brat." She stormed off and started to clank the dishes loudly, showing Steven her dismay.

This was one of many interactions with his parents that went awry. His father grew up in an era when children were meant to be seen and not heard, so any disagreement was viewed as disrespect. He used to punish Steven and yell at him whenever he was displeased with his behavior, shaming him and making him feel guilty for speaking up for himself.

With time, Steven learned that disagreements and conflict were harmful, and he avoided them at all costs. He became a people pleaser, going along with what everyone else wanted in order to protect the peace. Inside, he became resentful and angry, but he could never let that show on the outside.

He had to work on his people-pleasing tendencies in order to rise to leadership positions. He had to learn to deliver critical feedback and navigate disagreements with his team members.

But Julie's anger and personal character attacks reminded him of his mother's explosive anger. The younger parts of him that had learned to flee conflict and feel shame for speaking up were being activated.

Steven's reaction isn't uncommon. Many of us struggle with these types of dynamics, and therefore, we might avoid the hard conversations. Or if we have the hard conversations, we likely feel guilty or that we've done something wrong.

For better or for worse, we subconsciously mirror what was modeled for us when we were growing up. Our earliest observations stick with us until we learn a different way of being. The good news is that having an awareness of how those interactions earlier in life influence your interactions now allows you to practice a healthier way of showing up.

As you read on, think about how people handled difficult dynamics in your home when you were growing up. These experiences inform how you navigate workplace dynamics today.

✧

A few of us were lucky enough to grow up with relationships that modeled healthy conflict resolution. If it wasn't your caregivers modeling this, then it might have been your friends, coaches, teachers, or neighbors.

We saw them have a disagreement, but they didn't avoid, blow up, or snipe. They felt angry and frustrated, which is a natural human response, but they didn't take it out on the other person. Instead, they expressed their anger in a calm, direct manner and then had a discussion to come to a place of compromise and resolution. They didn't allow resentment and contempt to build; they saw the value in repairing the relationship.

Some families respond to conflict by sweeping issues under the rug. Nothing is ever wrong because nothing ever gets discussed or resolved. Difficult conversations are viewed as too uncomfortable, so they're avoided completely. These are the families that perpetuate the notion that "everything is fine" even when it's clearly not. Anyone who tries to address the issue directly is met with resistance and denial.

These families just flip a switch and go back to acting like nothing ever happened. A minimization takes place, and this makes it seem like the issue at hand isn't that big of a deal. Like when you tell your parent you're mad at them for embarrassing you in front of your friends, and they change the subject to what's for dinner or the weekend plans.

These family dynamics are often mistaken for being healthy because conflict is not overt. No one is screaming or yelling in the home, so it feels like all is well. But behind the scenes, issues and resentment grow until one day, the parents divorce, seemingly out of nowhere. Or they start sleeping in different rooms and putting both emotional and physical distance between each other.

This type of avoidance shows up in your workplace dynamics when people do not ask for critical feedback or skirt delivering it. Glossing over the issues feels safer than tackling them head-on, because addressing the underlying problems exposes you to being criticized or having to deal with someone who is upset.

Other families might address issues, but they do it in a

passive-aggressive manner. Nothing is discussed directly; instead, it's hinted at or spoken about in snipes. When one parent is unhappy with the other parent's lack of follow-through on loading the dishwasher, for example, they don't come out and say that. They say to their kid within earshot of the other parent, "I'm so sorry I was late picking you up from soccer practice today, Joe. I would have gotten there on time, but I had to spend an extra thirty minutes washing and loading up the dishes into the dishwasher. If only I had help around here."

These types of passive-aggressive remarks teach people that the best way to communicate is by ridiculing the other person in an indirect way. What is needed is never asked for, and it's assumed the other person will just pick up on how to behave.

This type of passive-aggression shows up in how you deliver feedback or ask for help. If a colleague isn't pulling their weight on a project, instead of directly saying, "Hey, I'm going to need help putting together the Excel sheets for this project," you might say, "I've been working on these spreadsheets for six hours, and I just can't figure them out. I don't know how I'm going to find time to get the rest of the project done."

The hope is that the colleague will jump in and say, "Oh, I'm great at spreadsheets, let me handle it." But often, the expectation and reality don't match up. Not being direct about what you want lessens the likelihood that you'll get what you need.

If you have to give criticism about an employee's tardiness but you're used to hinting, you might say something along the lines of, "Because we started our meeting late, I don't have time to discuss that upcoming project. I have back-to-back meetings and my day is running ten minutes behind now."

The employee will pick up on your frustration, but they won't necessarily get a sense that their tardiness is a long-term issue that needs addressing.

Instead, being direct and saying, "I understand that you got caught up with your work before our meeting, but I've noticed this happen a few times recently. It's important that we start our meetings on time so you get the full thirty minutes to discuss your goals. If you could please plan to join right at eleven a.m., that would be great."

Without directly expressing what you need and receiving the outcomes you deserve, bitterness takes hold. Unfortunately, we can't blame other people for not being able to read our minds. Being assertive and direct is a skill we need to learn and practice so we can undo some of the conditioning from earlier in life.

Remember, clear is kind.

Neurodivergent Tip

Individuals diagnosed with autism, ADHD, and other forms of neurodivergence often have difficulties reading between the lines. We tend to take people at face value, and hidden meanings can be lost on us.

Tarik was always a direct person who was blunt in his feedback to the team. If he didn't think an idea could work, he would say that in a respectful way but without mincing words. His directness was sometimes misinterpreted as aggression by his colleagues, and they started to pull away from him. No one shared with Tarik that they were offended by his directness, and instead they tried to passively let him know by avoiding him.

The team's discontent did not register in Tarik's mind. He figured that if people had a problem with him, they'd talk to him about it, so these dynamics went on for months until Tarik found himself isolated on the team.

One day, one of Tarik's friends on the team candidly shared with him. He talked about how Tarik's bluntness had rubbed people the wrong way and that they felt he was negative toward them. Tarik was stunned. He had assumed that people appreciated his honesty, but clearly this wasn't the case. He thanked his friend for being direct with him and decided to address the issue head-on.

In the next team meeting, Tarik made it a point to take accountability and apologize for upsetting people. He expressed that sometimes he could be overly honest and that he'd be more mindful of how he communicated feedback with others.

He also asked that team members come to him right away if he said or did something that was upsetting. He would never want to offend anyone, but he needed direct communication to know what was landing and what might not have landed.

Directly expressing how you feel and if something bothers you is key so guesswork isn't needed to know where the relationship stands. If you can be clear in your expectations and in what works versus what doesn't work, it will go a long way toward forging connection between you and your neurodivergent colleagues.

If you're the one who has accidentally offended folks at work, give yourself some grace. It takes time to learn people's communication preferences, and it varies from person to person. We often take it personally or start to shame spiral when someone addresses an issue, thinking that they must hate us or that we suck at communication, but it's a skill that we're constantly refining.

Part of learning to attune involves adapting to people's individual feedback and styles, and while some prefer a no-fluff, direct approach, others may need a feedback sandwich, where you lead with what's going well, then provide criticism, and finally end with more of what they're doing well.

It's okay to check in to see how your communication has landed. This can give you further guidance on whether to shift or maintain.

Chapter 3

Reacting Versus Responding: Understanding Triggers and Reactions

IT FELT LIKE her eyes were staring into my soul. She sat there silently, waiting for my response to her interrogation as the other group members watched uncomfortably.

She repeated, "Why would you choose to say and do that? That's not the right way. You're doing it wrong. You're being too direct. It feels like you're trying to prove your knowledge, and that's not what I'm looking for."

My supervisor was talking about the way I was teaching a student. I thought I was being helpful and supportive, but clearly, she had a different opinion.

I froze and mustered a response. "Uhh," I said as I stumbled along while trying to find my words. "I asked her the follow-up questions we talked about, but she kept saying 'I don't know.' I felt we were at a standstill, and I figured this was my time to teach instead of continuing with the Socratic dialogue."

Silence coupled with headshakes and a look of disapproval confirmed that my approach was wrong.

In an exasperated voice she said, "No. NO! You don't accept 'I don't know' as an answer. You have to push and pull out what they know. I'm not looking for you to just bombard them with information and give them the answers. I want you to extract what they know and manage your own anxiety when they tell you 'I don't know.' I'm not sure why this is so difficult for you to grasp."

I started feeling hot. I anxiously bopped my leg. It was so embarrassing that I was getting called out like this in front of the whole group of my colleagues. I could feel tears welling up in my eyes, and I quickly turned my camera off to dab them away.

I wasn't the only one to experience this. I witnessed every other person in the group have their own moment of being targeted. They too started to either tear up or shut down. Their reactions showed me that I wasn't being too sensitive. The actual problem was our supervisor's callous delivery.

That embarrassed feeling was so familiar. I felt like a total failure. Obviously I sucked at this, and I would never be good at teaching people. Even when I was trying so hard to apply what my supervisor was imparting, it still wasn't good enough. She might have been right, but her delivery triggered me.

My mind flashed back to many times staying late after school, trying to figure out my math homework. There I was, trying my best to understand algebra and solve for *x*, but I just wasn't getting it right, so I asked my teacher for help.

No matter how many times I tried to follow what they were saying, I kept getting it wrong. It felt like I was too dumb to pick it up. "You're not listening, Nidhi. Pay attention. This is how you do it." I'd try again and again, but it was still wrong. The frustrations mounted. My shame grew. I could feel my body getting hot. The leg shakes intensified as I started to shut down. The tears started flowing. Embarrassed and feeling like a failure, I'd run to the bathroom to cry alone.

Then, it clicked. My supervisor reminded me of my algebra teacher. She was terse, impatient, and quick to call me out in front of everyone else without any consideration for how I would feel. She became a huge trigger for me, and when I tried to express how I learn best—by not getting embarrassed in front of the group—she insisted that she wasn't the problem, I was.

Triggers are simply stimuli that elicit a reaction. Notice that the definition of a trigger doesn't say a stimulus that elicits a *response*. Triggers elicit a *reaction*.

Reactions are actions that are taken as a result of stimuli. The way we feel emotionally, physically, and cognitively in relationship to the trigger informs how we react in that situation.

Reactions are instantaneous and instinctual. They just kind of happen. The rational part of our brain, the prefrontal cortex, is offline when we are triggered, so the alarm system of the brain, the amygdala, takes over. This is when we tend to default to the fight, flight, freeze, or fawn reactions I referenced in chapter 1.

Different work situations can be triggering. Whether it's being excluded by team members going out to lunch, getting reprimanded by your boss, sensing that someone doesn't like you, or being micromanaged and controlled, you will have a reaction that is often strong and sometimes irrational.

These reactions often feel disproportionate to what's happening, as you saw in both my story above and Steven's story in chapter 2. It doesn't mean your feelings aren't valid or that the situation is acceptable, but big feelings rise to the surface quickly, and those feelings influence your reaction.

Responses are different. Responses are more rational and measured. They come from a grounded place, so you can choose how you want to show up.

When you're responding appropriately, your prefrontal cortex, the rational decision-making center, takes the lead by helping you stay in what's called your "wise mind." You're not overly rational or overly emotional; you're coming from a neutral, centered place. The rational and emotional perspectives are balanced, and your nervous system is calmer.

When I told my supervisor that I would benefit from a different approach, that was a response on my end. I'd practiced how I wanted to convey the message, and I was thoughtful in my approach. I remember taking deep breaths before I logged in for our meeting and making sure I didn't come from either an overly emotional or a too rational place.

What she said to me was actually a defensive reaction, not a response. She didn't take time to even consider my perspective or see the possibility that she could have an area for improvement. Instead, she immediately jumped to invalidating my feelings and blaming me for my reaction. It was crystal clear; this was a moment of misattunement.

We all have triggers that are bound to show up at work. The goal isn't to rid ourselves of triggers altogether. Rather, we're working toward creating space between the trigger and the reaction so we can choose how to respond versus reacting impulsively.

If we work in environments that are highly triggering, it not only affects us, but it also affects the outcomes for the people we're serving.

A 2024 research study published by the National Institutes of Health (NIH) reviewed the impact of triggers on health-care workers and their interactions with their patients. The researchers looked at several categories of emotional triggers, including patient and family factors, patient safety events and their repercussions, workplace toxicity, traumatic events, work overload, and a lack of supervisory support for teams.[1]

They found that certain types of emotions experienced in reaction to a trigger, such as fear, anger, and guilt, were correlated with negative effects on patient care and, ultimately, patient safety.

Having safe environments where all parties are emotionally regulated is critical to providing high-quality care to clients and customers. Without psychological safety and the tools to manage difficult emotions, employees are unable to perform at their highest level. Outcomes suffer, and it's bad for business.

That certainly held true for me. I became less confident in myself as a teacher and started to second-guess everything I did. When I was with a student, my anxiety was so high that I wasn't able to be fully present, as I was too worried about whether I was doing it right. My supervisor's voice was in my head, actively sabotaging me. I have no doubt that the quality of services I provided during that time was negatively impacted by my persistently being triggered.

I did end up going to therapy to work through some of my past experiences that were being triggered, but ultimately, even my therapist pointed out that healing cannot happen in toxic environments. She encouraged me to reflect on whether I could truly thrive with these types of dynamics at play, and I came to the conclusion that I could not. I made the tough decision to take a step back and focus on other goals in order to protect my own peace, and I'm so grateful I did.

Neurodivergent Tip

Many of the people around you have experienced some sort of trauma, whether that is a lack of connection in childhood, emotional abuse, bullying, or feeling othered. Their past experiences have shaped the way they move through the world. Or maybe you're the one who has experienced trauma, and interactions at work can be challenging.

As you learned in chapter 1, there are four trauma responses: fight, flight, freeze, and fawn. People with a trauma history are often moving through the world in a hypervigilant way, as they are constantly on guard and scanning for threats. Communication with people who have experienced trauma can require adaptation, as they can be sensitive to any feelings of abandonment, rejection, and harm.

For example, people who learned to fawn as their survival response earlier in life struggle with conflict and disagreements later in life. Growing up, many of them were in physical or emotional danger when they disagreed with others, so as adults, they have difficulties saying what they truly think or want. They've learned to abandon their own needs in order to meet others' needs, and they avoid disapproval at all costs. These are the folks who tend to go with the flow, appeasing everyone around them. Their past experiences have taught them that disagreements equal conflict, and that conflict can lead to harm or abandonment.

If this describes you, then you'll want to work on making your thoughts, feelings, and needs explicit. Remember, you are allowed to express what you need, because if you don't, resentment starts to brew. You can start with low-stakes situations, like voicing a preference for where you and the team go for lunch or sharing an idea at a team meeting. These smaller steps help you see that it's safe to speak up for what you desire.

When you are interacting with people pleasers at work, it is important to reassure them that they are allowed to have different opinions from the group. It may take them some time to truly trust in that, but eventually, they will start expressing their thoughts more openly. In addition, asking them for feedback one-on-one is likely less intimidating than asking them to share their perspective in a group. Take the time to let them know that their ideas are valued and that the way the team grows is by having a multitude of approaches to solving a problem.

It is also vital that you do not guilt or shame anyone, but you want to be especially careful doing this to people who have a trauma history. Any inkling of guilt often leads to people with a trauma history going against their own needs to meet yours, and this will eventually breed resentment. Guilt in conversations can sound like "I know that you scheduled this two-week vacation, and I want you to be able to take time off, but Jessie is going to have to cover your work while you're gone. I'm sure we'll figure it out, but it'll be a bit stressful for us all."

Guilt is also manipulative and passive-aggressive, so you want to avoid using that tactic altogether. Instead, just let the person know, "I know that you have a two-week vacation scheduled, and I wanted to let you know that we have a coverage plan in place for the time you're gone. We'll be sure to update you on everything that happened once you come back." You are still communicating that there is a coverage plan, but you are leaving out the guilt and hardship that this will cause the team. If you want people to take care of themselves and prioritize well-being so they can perform well at work, then you cannot make them feel bad for doing so.

If you're the person who tends to feel guilty when advocating for what you need, then this will take deliberate practice to unlearn. One helpful reframe is remembering that you cannot control how other people react. The guilt might set in because you fear you've disappointed someone or let them down. In these moments, you can remind yourself that they're allowed to feel how they feel and that you can't manage others' emotions for them.

Remember, by attempting to protect others' feelings, you're neglecting your own.

Chapter 4

Know Thyself
+
Keep Calm and Carry On

BEFORE WE CAN excel at leading others, we need to lead ourselves. That's why we dove into the importance of triggers and reactions in the previous chapters, and now we're going to dig deeper into uncovering your own triggers and reactions.

I know what you might be thinking: "Isn't that what therapy is for?" Doing this work isn't reserved for the therapist's office, although you might benefit from exploring what you uncover with a professional.

It's an essential part of showing up as the team member and leader who is effective at managing your emotions so you can connect and communicate well with others.

Without self-mastery, relationships at work suffer.

Know Thyself

It was the slap heard around the world.

I think most of us remember watching or hearing about the 2022 Oscars with the infamous heated exchange between Will Smith and Chris Rock. Rock made a joke about Smith's wife, Jada Pinkett Smith, and her buzz cut, saying he was looking forward to seeing her in *GI Jane 2*.

The joke was in especially bad taste because Pinkett Smith had candidly and vulnerably shared about her struggles with hair loss and alopecia. As Pinkett Smith rolled her eyes at the *GI Jane 2* joke, Smith quickly hopped on the stage and slapped Rock, telling him to "Keep my wife's name out of your f*cking mouth."

Stunned, the world watched this unfold on live TV, or we watched it on replay later.

What's interesting about Smith's reaction is that while it seemed to come out of nowhere, and seemed to be completely out of character, there were likely cues that led to his explosion. His reaction is actually what happens to so many of the clients I serve. Emotions go from zero to one hundred in seconds, and before you know it, an explosive, triggered reaction comes out.

Now of course, I have to preface this analysis by saying that I don't personally know Will Smith, Jada Pinkett Smith, or Chris Rock, nor was I in the room that night. But what I do know is that in my more than thirteen years as a therapist, explosions and big reactions are rarely totally out of left field.

Later, it came out that Rock had made multiple digs at Smith and Pinkett Smith in the past. It seems like there was a buildup of emotion and anger that preceded this interaction.

When you watch the video from that night, you see Rock make the joke and Smith seem to be laughing it off. But subtle shifts in Smith's facial expressions, even while he's laughing, indicate that he's perturbed by the comment. Clearly, the anger was quickly building before he walked up onstage to assault Rock.

Then, when the camera pans back to Smith after he returns to his seat, you can see the aggravation. His eyes are full of rage and laser focused on Rock, his lips are downturned, and he repeatedly yells to Rock to "Keep my wife's name out of your f*cking mouth!" with an aggressive tone. It's as if he's seeing red and is having tunnel vision, forgetting his wife and the audience behind him.

This is a perfect example of how quickly emotions can escalate and why it's critical to *know thyself.*

In his public apology, Smith stated, "Jokes at my expense are a part of the job, but a joke about Jada's medical condition was too much for me to bear, and I reacted emotionally."

After the fact, Smith was able to recognize that his reaction was inappropriate and intense, but in the moment, his brain was telling him that he needed to defend his wife, even if that meant assaulting Rock.

Not having that kind of rational thought in the moment cost him big time.

As of April 8, 2022, Smith is not permitted to attend any Academy events for the next ten years, including the Academy Awards. His reputation suffered in an instant, and he's had to apologize repeatedly to his children, his family, and the world in order to mitigate the damage done.

If he had been able to slow things down in that moment, recognize that he was being triggered, and then calm himself down out of that fight response, the outcome likely would have been different.

What does this celebrity story have to do with you and how situations play out in the workplace? If you can't recognize your own triggers or the signs that you're escalating, it can cost you majorly, too.

I've seen people have HR complaints and investigations against them for outbursts, or get fired for insubordination, and witnessed how these types of emotional reactions can sabotage one's career.

Long before you experience an emotion like anger, sadness, or embarrassment, your body and brain send you cues that something is awry.

Physical sensations, emotions, thoughts, and behaviors are in a feedback loop, and each impacts the others. However, according to the James-Lange theory, before you experience an emotion, your brain shifts your physiological state, which then leads to the emotional reaction.[1]

Further research has found that physiological changes can be perceived as feelings via interoception, or the ability to sense and interpret bodily signals, such as heart rate and pain.[2] This physiological information contributes to emotions as well as to emotion regulation, survival, and reproduction.

When your physiological state changes, it directly impacts the chemicals and neural activity in the brain, which then influences your cognitive and emotional states.

Chemicals like cortisol and adrenaline are released when your brain and body sense a sudden negative shift. This then leads to your sympathetic nervous system, which is involved in engaging fight, flight, freeze, and fawn mode, informing how you perceive the situation emotionally and cognitively.

For example, receiving an out-of-the-blue meeting invite

from HR after you heard through the grapevine that people were getting laid off in other departments will likely cause your muscles to tense, your heart rate to increase, and your body to perspire. You might notice your body feels hot and your hands become shaky. These physical reactions then lead to the perception of fear.

If you can catch the physiological reactions early enough, then you are more able to calm down before the emotion fully takes hold.

The best way to achieve this is to notice those early signals from your body and **RESET**.

***R* is for Reaction.** When you have a strong reaction to a situation, take a moment to pause. Observe what's happening in your body. Your body will give you the first signals that something is awry. Is your body tensing up? Are your shoulders hunched? Is your breathing quickening? Is your heart racing? Detecting these cues helps you identify the ways your mind and body react when stressed. As you develop this skill set, you'll be able to recognize the early signs that you're having a strong reaction, and you'll learn how to thwart it. Noticing your reactions is the first step to interrupting your reactions so you can approach the situation more logically.

***E* is for Emotions.** You've observed your initial physiological reaction, so you can now pause to name the emotions that are coming up for you. Label what's going on emotionally so that you can start to calm your nervous system. Are you feeling fearful? Disappointed? Numb? Exposed? Dr. Daniel Siegel's research found that if we can name our emotions, then we can tame our emotions.[3] When you're able to connect with your emotional experience, your brain starts to better understand why your body is in an activated state. Don't try to logic your way through and understand the "why" behind the reaction just yet—we'll get there shortly.

***S* is for Soothe.** Now that you've noticed your physiological and emotional reactions, it's time to soothe your nervous system. I cover this more later in the chapter, but some techniques include changing your breathing so you take in fuller breaths, gently rubbing your arms to ground yourself in the present, and stretching your body so you can ease body tension. This helps your nervous system shift from a sympathetic, or stressed, state to a parasympathetic, or restful, state. Remember, you can't think through the underlying reasons for why you're reacting strongly until you calm down your nervous system. Your prefrontal cortex, or the part of your brain in charge of logical reasoning, decision-making, and determining appropriate responses, is offline when your mind and body sense a threat. Trying to think through the situation at this point often results in frustration. Calm body = calm mind, so soothe and then synthesize.

***E* is for Explore.** Now that you're calm, take a moment to connect with what evoked this reaction. In the example above, when you received the meeting invite from HR out of the blue, you jumped to negative conclusions with little evidence backing up that response. It's normal to feel nervous, but if you're feeling panicky and having a full-blown anxiety attack, then it's important to explore where that's coming from. How does this moment feel familiar to you? Have you been caught off guard with bad news before? Have you previously had the rug pulled out from underneath you? Remember, the present connects to the past, and identifying these past-present connections helps you make sense of your reactions in the here and now.

***T* is for Tell.** Once you get a sense of what's happening underneath your reaction, tell someone you trust about your experience. Sharing your experience with another person helps you feel more regulated and it also aids in feeling less alone. Too often, you may try to keep your experience to yourself out of embarrassment or not wanting to burden others, but this only amplifies your feelings of isolation. Connection is essential for healing and repair. Just be sure that you share your experiences with people who are validating and good at holding space. Confiding in someone who is a poor listener, makes it about them, or invalidates your experience can cause you to feel triggered all over again.

All this happens quite quickly, and it takes practice to recognize what's happening inside. This holds especially true if you've gotten skilled at disconnecting from your feelings or just pushing through them.

I've noticed that for many of my high-achieving corporate clients, ***stillness feels unsafe***.

They never slow down or truly rest, because when they do, all the feelings they were suppressing bubble up to the surface.

The anxiety, the stress, the exhaustion, and the unhappiness that they staved off for months begin to flood them, and they feel so uncomfortable with those feelings that they numb them with more work and more tasks. They'll put energy toward anything that gives them a sense of control so they can ignore the inner turmoil.

They're on vacation yet they're checking emails constantly and responding to work calls. When their family tells them to disconnect from work, they compulsively organize the hotel room or start getting agitated that everyone is just sitting around on the beach not doing anything. These are the folks who live by the ethos that rest and recuperation are earned only after the work is done, except the work is never done.

This type of avoidance not only takes a toll emotionally, it also takes a toll physically.

The good news is that creating this mind-body connection is a skill anyone can develop. It just takes diligent, daily practice.

In order to build this skill set, you'll first have to connect with what your body feels like when it's calm.

Do you notice that certain muscles relax, like your shoulders? Are you able to take deeper breaths and expand your chest more easily? Is your resting heart rate lower?

I use my Apple Watch or another fitness tracker to monitor how my body feels on lower-stress days versus high-stress days. Usually, my resting heart rate is almost ten beats per minute slower on days when I'm relaxed compared to days when I'm stressed.

Then, when you are feeling stressed or emotionally activated, pause and notice what's happening. I'd recommend starting by observing for thirty seconds at a time, especially when you're first trying this.

Intentionally observe the physical shifts that happen, from quickened breathing to chest tightness, headaches, slumped posture, stomach aches, or muscle tension. These will become the indicators that will tip you off that you're feeling unsettled in your mind and body.

Then pause and just allow these sensations to exist. You don't need to distract or look away; just be with them. You can observe, saying to yourself, "I'm noticing that my shoulders are slumped. My gut feels like it's in knots." No judgment. Just observation.

Sit with the discomfort. Do this for thirty seconds and then build to forty-five seconds, then sixty seconds, and so on. You might feel the desire to distract yourself or even doomscroll to shift your attention away from what's happening within, but when you stick with it, you're building your distress tolerance and expanding your window of tolerance, meaning you're better able to stay calm and regulated during stressful situations.

The more that you can strengthen your distress tolerance, the better you're able to be in tune with your inner world, and the more likely you'll be to make good decisions in how you respond to situations that trigger you.

The biggest mistake I see people make is that when they start feeling the discomfort of an emotion, they immediately try to think through what's causing them to feel that way. This often leads to them feeling frustrated and even more anxious because they're unable to immediately make meaning of their experience.

My advice is that calm body = calm mind.

Once your body is calmer and your emotions are better managed in the moment, then you can explore what you were thinking that led you to feel that way. You'll want to explore what precipitated the event, what occurred during the event, and what happened after the event.

If you're one of the people I referenced a moment ago who keeps yourself busy because stillness feels unsafe, then just notice what thoughts and feelings come up when you're in a calm state.

Maybe you're thinking "I'm lazy" because you're not achieving something in that moment, or maybe you're thinking "I'm incompetent" because there is so much more to be done and you just can't power through. It might even be that you feel guilty for not responding to the email immediately or not taking those few free minutes to wash the dishes because it feels like it might make more work for others.

I can remember a number of times when I felt uncomfortable emotions and they blindsided me. I know I'm a therapist, but I'm a human who struggles sometimes, too.

I'd be sitting on my couch, watching TV and resting, when all of a sudden, my heart rate would shoot up to 115 beats per minute, my palms would start getting sweaty, and I would feel like I couldn't get enough air into my lungs. Panicked and stressed, I'd lie down, take some deep breaths, and try to ground myself.

Once my heart rate came back down to the seventies and eighties and my breathing slowed, I'd take a few minutes to recall what I was thinking and feeling in that moment. My physiological response was creating the emotional response of anxiety.

It turns out, subconsciously, while I was watching one of my favorite trashy reality TV shows, my thoughts were turning to how much work I had to get done. I was feeling like a procrastinator. I'd begin worrying that I wouldn't be able to get all the work completed, and my mind would be crafting the emails I was behind on sending.

For me, in those moments, stillness felt unsafe. The physiological escalation combined with the emotion of anxiety and the racing thoughts would lead to a panic episode.

When I think back on the times that I was burning out at work, there were months of physiological signs that I ignored. I was constantly sick, my inflammation markers were high, and I kept getting these weird zaps in my chest that would cause my heart to race.

The chest zaps got to the point that I saw a cardiologist to be sure something wasn't off with my heart rhythm. After wearing a Holter monitor, getting EKGs done, having an echocardiogram of my heart completed, and getting a CT scan of my cardiovascular system, it turns out it was likely stress and anxiety related.

The mind and body are interconnected and intertwined, as Bessel van der Kolk indicates in the title of his book, *The Body Keeps the Score.*

Now that I'm consistently practicing getting more in tune with my own internal experiences, I'm noticing that my anxiety is much better managed. I'm equipped to catch the shoulder tension and heart racing using the RESET technique before it leads to full-on panic. And I feel more empowered to navigate stress.

Keep Calm and Carry On

The house of cards was rapidly collapsing, and the CEO seemed to have no idea how to keep up the charade.

Back in 2001, one of the biggest scandals to hit the business world occurred within a company whose name became synonymous with corruption: Enron.

According to *Forbes* magazine, Jeffrey Skilling became the CEO of the Enron Corporation in early 2001 and then quit four months before the company filed for bankruptcy. In one particular call with Richard Grubman, an analyst with Highfields Capital Management, Skilling couldn't explain how he didn't have financial documents from Enron.

During the call with Skilling, Grubman exclaimed, "You're the only financial institution that can't produce a balance sheet or cash flow statement with their earnings!"

Grubman didn't know it at the time, but Enron's earnings were nonexistent, so Skilling was continually dodging providing information that reflected the company's true earnings.

Flustered and unable to come up with a valid reason for the lack of transparency, Skilling responded, flustered, "You, you, you . . . well . . . uh . . . thank you very much. We appreciate it . . . *asshole*!"

Skilling's temper continued to intensify, exposing his uneasiness with Enron's financial future. During testimony to Congress in 2002, Skilling regretfully said, "If I could go back and redo things, I would not, now, have used the term that I used."

In 2006, he was convicted of conspiracy, insider trading, making false statements, and securities fraud.[4]

Blowups like this happen all the time in the business world, and they're the reactions to triggers, like we discussed in the earlier "Know Thyself" section. In this case, Skilling's trigger was the fear of getting caught in a lie and needing to cover up mistakes. But not every blowup has to be under such extreme circumstances.

Steve Jobs, one of the founders of Apple, allegedly was such a perfectionist that he'd become combative toward his employees. When he was an executive at NeXT Computers, a computer manufacturer started to explain the design for the computer's outside shell, which would cost two hundred dollars.

Before the man could complete his sentence, Jobs cut him off and told him he wouldn't allow the part to cost more than twenty dollars. He then reportedly began screaming wildly for four minutes, which I'd imagine frightened the employees. The shell ended up costing two hundred dollars, despite Jobs's explosive reaction.

Another employee reflected, "Tell Steve you can't do something because it violates the laws of physics, and he says that's not good enough."[5]

For Jobs, the idea that something can't be done, or perhaps the word *no*, was a trigger. His perfectionism convinced him that anything could be accomplished if you just pushed hard enough to make it happen. This mindset led to distrust and a toxic culture within NeXT Computers.

Being able to stay emotionally regulated is critical for job satisfaction and happiness at work. A 2020 study aimed to better understand the experience of affect, or emotions, at work, and examined whether self-regulation of emotions is related to job satisfaction.[6]

The researchers conducted a quantitative diary study in which they had participants in an MBA program at a major university respond to a survey about demographic information and ratings of emotion regulation behavior as well as trait affect, or their emotional state. The participants were professional staff, team leaders, and executive managers. They completed these diaries over nine days, and the researchers studied the correlation between their emotional state, their ability to emotionally regulate, and their job satisfaction.

Better emotional regulation was related to positive feelings while working, thereby increasing the likelihood of positive judgments toward the job and the organization. The extent to which employees felt satisfied at work depended on whether they were able to sustain positive feelings and reduce negative ones while working.[7]

A multitude of skills can help you get out of the negative emotional and cognitive loop that contributes to feeling dysregulated in the workplace. In the previous section, we discussed being able to recognize when your physiology and emotional state are becoming activated, and now, we'll dive into what to do when you start to notice you're in a heightened state.

Orienting to Safety

The first and most foundational skill is to establish safety. Remember, when you're in fight, flight, freeze, or fawn mode, your brain, specifically your amygdala, is perceiving a threat to your safety. Your body gets ready to mobilize, slowing down digestion, sending blood to your extremities, and tensing your muscles. In order to start calming down, you have to prove to your brain and body that you are safe.

The eyes, ears, and neck are the orientation centers for the brain, because they are in charge of scanning your environment for threats. When you're first noticing the physiological signs of distress, turn your head from side to side and scan your environment with your eyes and ears, making note if there are any active threats to your safety in this exact moment. If there are not, then you might say to yourself, "I am safe in this moment. Nothing is here to harm me or impact my survival."

Four-Seven-Eight Breathing

Once you've established physical safety, then it's time to start calming down your nervous system by managing your breathing. The pace of your breathing also sends signals to your brain about danger, stress, and anxiety, which in turn activates fight, flight, or freeze. If your breathing is quickened, then your nervous system tells your brain that there are threats present, which releases adrenaline and further quickens your breathing. The amygdala, which processes emotions, is particularly sensitive to these breathing signals and can trigger a fear response. Because you're in this hyperaroused state, you can't think clearly and you will have difficulties focusing.

The four-seven-eight breathing technique, designed by Dr. Andrew Weil, promotes relaxation and stress reduction by regulating the nervous system. It will help you shift from a stressed state to a calm state relatively quickly, allowing you to feel more present and grounded. It'll also encourage you to focus and think more rationally through a stressful situation. Research shows that this breathing technique also can help you improve your heart rate variability and blood pressure.[8]

For this technique, you'll breathe in through your nose for four seconds, hold in the breath for seven seconds, and exhale through your mouth for eight seconds. You'll do this as many times as you need to until you start noticing your breathing calm down and your heart rate slowing. I practice this technique regularly, especially when I notice that my heart is racing or my body is feeling tense. You can even visualize yourself breathing into the parts of your body that are tense, allowing that stress to melt away.

Body Scan

Many signs of stress are stored in our bodies, but we get accustomed to them and don't notice how much tension we're carrying. An easy daily practice that you can integrate even while sitting at your desk is a short, three-minute body scan. This technique assists in identifying places where your body is carrying stress so you can intentionally release it.

I recommend reading this exercise all the way through and then sitting down to practice it on your own. You could also have someone read this to you as you practice it, or you can watch my LinkedIn Learning course "Tips to Enhance Emotional Intelligence with Calming Exercises," which guides you through these exercises.

First, rate your current level of stress on a scale of zero to ten, with ten being the most stressed you've ever been. Now, sit comfortably in a chair, allowing your back to rest against the chair's back. Be sure your feet are planted firmly on the ground beneath you, and observe the connection you have to the earth. Take three to five of the four-seven-eight breaths, and allow your heart rate and breathing to shift into a calmer state. Notice how it feels to be present in this moment.

Starting with the top of your head, notice your scalp, forehead, and face. Observe any tension you're holding, and intentionally tense those parts of your head. If you notice stress in your forehead, tense those muscles and then quickly release them. Scrunch your face if you notice muscle tension and then quickly release those muscles. Notice the shift that happens when you go from tense to calm.

Focus your attention on your shoulders, arms, and hands.

Notice if your shoulders are hunched or if they're up high by your ears. These are signs that your shoulders are carrying tension and the weight of your stress. Observe your arms and hands, gauging whether they are tensed or relaxed. Now, lift your shoulders up toward your ears and then quickly allow them to fall to their normal, lowered position. Then ball your fists and tense your hands and forearms for a few seconds before un-balling your fists and relaxing your arms. Pay attention to the difference between when your muscles are tense and when they are relaxed.

Finally, shift your attention to your legs and feet. Check in and see whether your feet feel tired from carrying you through all the stressors of the day. Lift your feet from flat on the ground to tense and up on your tiptoes. Tense your calf muscles for a few seconds and then quickly release. Curl your toes for a few seconds, noticing the tension, and then quickly release.

Sit for about thirty seconds, noticing how it feels to have connected to your body, part by part. Observe the shifts that happened when you intentionally focused on tensing and releasing your muscles, and notice any differences in your stress levels. Take a moment to rate your stress levels on that one-to-ten scale. Are you feeling calmer and more regulated now?

You can use this technique at work or at home. It will help you get your body back on track.

Five Senses Grounding

The five senses grounding technique is a simple one that helps you refocus on the here and now in moments of stress and anxiety. So much of anxiety is rooted in past worries or future concerns, so being able to ground in the present helps alleviate that anxiety response.

For this exercise, you'll notice five things you can see, four things you can touch, three things you can hear, two things you can smell, and one thing you can taste.

Get comfortable by sitting in a chair and placing your feet flat on the floor. Take a look around where you are, and start noticing your surroundings.

First, name five things you can see. Notice the paintings on the wall, the color of the carpet, the lights in the corner, the chair you're sitting on, and the computer on your desk, for example.

Next, name four things you can touch. This can include pens, your phone, the floor beneath you, your keyboard, your coffee cup, or anything in your vicinity that you can make physical contact with.

Now, name three things you can hear. Maybe you have the fan running, you might hear the chatter of colleagues down the hallway, or you might even have music playing on your computer.

Then, name two things you can smell. You might smell your lunch heating up in the microwave or the scent of the candles in your home office. I always love connecting to the smell of my coffee brewing as I get ready for the day.

Finally, name one thing you can taste. You might be chewing gum or drinking coffee, or maybe you have the lingering remnants of your lunch on your tongue. Take a moment to connect with what you're tasting.

Settle into the stillness and calm that comes from being present in this moment. Notice whether your stress or anxiety has lessened as a result of completing this exercise.

The nicest element of this technique is that you can use it and no one knows that you're grounding yourself. I've used the five senses grounding technique during stressful sales calls or intense client sessions. It works well and isn't obvious to those around you, so you can keep it in your back pocket as a stealthy technique to use in moments of activation.

Calm/Safe Place

Visualization techniques are a cornerstone of mindfulness, and they can be a powerful way to manage your emotional state. As an Eye Movement Desensitization and Reprocessing (EMDR) therapist, consultant, and teacher, I've seen firsthand the power of using the Calm/Safe Place exercise to regulate emotions. Dr. Francine Shapiro, the inventor of EMDR, developed this technique to help clients quickly come down emotionally when experiencing distress. It is an important skill for improving your window of tolerance and changing your emotional state.

The premise of the exercise is that we can develop positive memory networks that we can recall instantaneously to go from a stressed state to a calm state. We reinforce these positive memory networks using butterfly tapping, which is a slow, back-and-forth tapping technique that enhances the images, emotions, and body sensations tied to the experience.

For this exercise, you'll want to think of a place either real or imagined where you feel calm and at peace. It could be your favorite beach, a mountain, a garden, or a place you'd like to visit one day. If you choose a place that you haven't been before, pull up a picture of this place on your phone or computer so you can better visualize the destination.

The caveats are that you can't have any negative associations with this place, and there can't be anyone else there alongside you.

We don't want negative associations because it taints the positive feelings tied to the experience, and we don't want to reinforce any negative feelings. We also don't want other people in our calm/safe place because our relationships with people are complicated. Even the healthiest relationships have moments of discord, so we want to uncomplicate the memory by visualizing the location with us in it by ourselves.

The other caveat is that if you have the tendency to dissociate, or disconnect from your emotions and body, then you'll want to do this exercise with a trained professional who can help you stay present. If you struggle with visualization, then use an image and look at that to make it more tangible.

Before we begin the exercise, visit nidhitewari.com and look at the diagram created by EMDR for Kids to learn and practice the butterfly hug. With your palms facing you, cross your hands and link your thumbs to form the body of the butterfly. Bring your butterfly to your chest, over your heart, so your fingertips (the butterfly wings) are touching your collarbones. Then slowly tap with your fingertips on your collarbones . . . right, left, right, left, right. You'll repeat this slowly six to eight times to strengthen the memory network that you're creating.

Once you have your calm/safe place identified, you'll want to start immersing yourself in the details of that place. First, select an image that represents your calm/safe place. Describe or write down what you see. If it's helpful, you can even draw your place to help you with visualizing it.

My calm/safe place is the train ride on the way to the World

Economic Forum in Davos, Switzerland. The conference was taking place in May the year I went, and I remember seeing the snowcapped Swiss Alps, the pristine waterfalls and rivers, and the lush greenery.

Next, as you connect with the image that represents your calm/safe place, observe the positive emotions that arise. Perhaps you're feeling at ease, rested, or peaceful. Notice where you experience these positive emotions in your body. Take a moment to register all the sights, sounds, smells, and sensations of being in your calm/safe place.

I remember feeling so peaceful and awestruck by the beauty that surrounded me on that train. I can still feel the soft, plush seats; smell the cappuccino being brewed onboard; and hear the sound of the train quietly chugging along. My shoulders relax and my chest feels much more expansive remembering back to that ride.

Once you have the image, positive emotions, body sensations, and all the elements of being in your calm/safe place in your mind, then begin the slow butterfly taps. Tap back and forth slowly six to eight times to strengthen that memory. Notice what comes up as you tap, and if you notice positive emotions, then do another set of eight to ten slow taps.

If you have any negative experiences, then stop and use the four-seven-eight breathing exercise to calm yourself down.

Now that you've enhanced your calm/safe place, come up with a word or a short phrase that will remind you of it and take you back there quickly. For me, my cue word for my calm/safe place is *Davos* because saying that word instantly takes me back to all the sights, sounds, smells, and sensations of watching the Swiss Alps go by from the train.

When you have your cue word in mind, bring back up the image, positive emotions, and positive body sensations, and repeat the cue word while doing the slow butterfly hug, tapping back and forth another six to eight times. This will help connect the cue word to your calm/safe place.

Without tapping, practice using your cue word to bring up your calm/safe place. Just repeating the word in your head should allow you to become reimmersed in all the positive elements of the experience.

Finally, let's put this technique to the test to ensure you're able to go from tense to calm. Think of a situation that's mildly distressing, on a scale of zero to ten, with ten being most distressing; we're looking for an experience that's a one or two. This might include getting stuck in traffic, running a few minutes late to a dinner out with friends, or coming up on a deadline. Maybe you feel anxious, annoyed, or upset. Notice the distressing emotions and where you experience them in your body.

Use your cue word to bring yourself back to your calm/safe place, and notice any positive shifts in your emotional state and body. Observe where the tension releases and whether you're feeling calmer. Think of something slightly more distressing, like a two or three on that zero-to-ten scale, and use your cue word to reevoke that calm/safe place. Again, notice any changes in your emotional state and body.

Now you have a calm/safe place you can access any time you feel stressed. I recommend practicing this technique in the morning, on your lunch break, or when you get home after work. Use this both when you're calm and when you're stressed. It's easier to remember to utilize this skill when you're stressed if you develop the skill while you're in a calmer state of mind.

Spiral Technique

Another research-backed technique created by Dr. Francine Shapiro is called the Spiral technique. This exercise allows you to shift a distressing emotion or experience relatively quickly. I've used it with clients, and I've practiced it myself in my own EMDR therapy sessions.

First, you'll bring up a slightly disturbing memory and concentrate on the body sensations that accompany it. Think back on the original event, and rate how distressing it feels to you now on that zero-to-ten scale.

Notice where you feel that distress in your body. You might notice that your gut feels like it's in knots or your chest feels tight. Concentrate on what you're feeling in your body, and visualize those feelings as a spiraling ball of energy. Observe whether the ball of energy is rotating clockwise or counterclockwise.

Then, focus on the feelings and switch the direction of the spiral from counterclockwise to clockwise, or vice versa. Observe the shift that happens as you change the direction of the rotation of the energy. For many people, they notice the distress start to dissipate and they feel a release from those feelings.

If this doesn't work for you, shift back into another skill, like four-seven-eight breathing, or use the five senses grounding technique to help bring you back to the present.

If you do get relief, then practice this skill with progressively more distressing memories, but try not to pick anything higher than a four or five on the zero-to-ten scale. The more that you utilize this tool, the easier it will be to access it when you're facing a moment of stress.

Name It to Tame It

When I attended TED2024 in Vancouver, I got the opportunity to connect with an iconic TED Talker at the party held on the last night, Dr. Jill Bolte Taylor. We both sat and talked for an hour about all things related to the brain and whole-brain living. She gave one of the most powerful TED Talks, called "My Stroke of Insight," during which she chronicles her journey as a brain researcher experiencing a stroke.

Bolte Taylor has devoted her life to researching the way emotions work, and through her research, she found that it only takes ninety seconds to identify an emotion and allow it to dissipate. Pausing for ninety seconds and labeling what you're feeling by saying, "I'm feeling nervous," or "I'm getting frustrated," reduces activity in the amygdala. Doing this allows you to regain control.

Bolte Taylor also discusses how there is a ninety-second chemical process that happens in the body, which then flushes out after those ninety seconds pass. Once those chemicals dissipate, you can exit that emotional loop. If you're still feeling distressing emotions like anger or fear after those ninety seconds, you can explore what thoughts are spiraling and reigniting that physiological reaction.[9]

Dr. Daniel Siegel echoes this same concept in his exercise Name It to Tame It. He states that when emotions arise, you can describe your internal state without rationalizing or judging what you're feeling. This process promotes integration by strengthening the brain's language capacities and connecting them to raw emotions in other parts of the brain.

Ignoring or avoiding these emotions only amplifies them, so be sure to lean in instead of away.

If you'd like me to guide you through the techniques outlined in this chapter, then check out my LinkedIn Learning course "Tips to Enhance Emotional Intelligence with Calming Exercises."

Neurodivergent Tip

It can be challenging to remember these tools in moments of stress, and neurodivergent folks tend to default to their conditioned responses.

For example, I worked with Mary in therapy, and because she had ADHD, she had the hardest time coming back to these interventions in the moment. She always felt caught off guard because her emotions escalated so quickly, and the window of opportunity to shift her physiological state was smaller than those of her neurotypical counterparts.

She needed tangible reminders to help her remember to practice these skills, so we utilized the reminders app on her iPhone as a way to schedule morning and evening moments for skill development.

Mary set an alarm that would go off during her lunch break so she could remember to pause, mindfully eat her food, and decompress before jumping back into the work left in her day. She also set an alarm for after work so that on her commute home, or when she left her home office to go downstairs, she had an opportunity to shed the stress of the day.

Practicing these emotional regulation skills in times when she was calm made a huge difference in her being able to remember to utilize them when she was in the midst of a conflict or in a moment of increased stress. She was able to see firsthand that these tools have an immediate benefit, and building them into her daily routine made a massive difference.

Mary also had a cheat sheet that listed these tools that she kept on the bulletin board in her cubicle, and she kept another copy on her fridge at home. That way, if she needed a more physical reminder or was too activated to think about what to do, she could easily check her list.

Having these resources available in your office or your common areas at work can be helpful for ensuring people are able to stay grounded. Creating quiet spaces for people to retreat to and decompress in can also be a way to provide the right circumstances for emotional regulation.

This is especially important for individuals who are neurodivergent, as being around stimulation and other people can feel overwhelming. Quiet spaces with items like noise-canceling headphones, soft blankets, and soothing fidget accessories can be of assistance, too.

Part II

Tuning In to Others

Now that you've learned how to understand your own emotional reactions and manage them in a healthy way, it's time to explore how to connect more effectively with your colleagues and teams.

Part II will cover the common pitfalls in interpersonal communications as well as strategies to bridge these divides. We'll explore examples of attuned and misattuned workplaces throughout history, and we'll glean lessons from what went well and what went sideways.

We'll also gain perspective on how we can shape the future of work in the age of AI in a way that still prioritizes humanity in the workplace.

We can't be people leaders without prioritizing people first, and that's what this section is all about.

Chapter 5

The Connection Gap

"Does anyone have any difficult client scenarios that they want to share?"

The Zoom call was silent. Everyone shifted in their chairs, their eyes scanned back and forth, and there wasn't a smile in sight. No one wanted to share their thoughts with Brandi. The silence seemed to drag on forever, and no one felt comfortable coming off of mute to share their struggles.

"If you can't share about your clients on this call, how are you going to problem-solve issues live with them in the future?"

Brandi was trying to motivate the team to share, but it came across as shaming, and it didn't work. Finally, someone piped up to break the awkward silence and Brandi began dissecting every word.

This was exactly why no one spoke up.

In the past, Brandi tended to jump on her team members if they misspoke or didn't know the correct answer. The spotlight shone brightly on whoever had the guts to speak up, and Brandi's response, an interrogation in front of the group, was an unintentional punishment for being courageous. She meant well, but the team felt totally disconnected from Brandi.

Brandi had been promoted into a leadership position ten years prior, and she rose in the ranks because of her keen eye and her ability to speak her mind bluntly and clearly. With the old guard, her approach was viewed as necessary and valuable in shaping up the team, and she was not one to mince words when she felt someone was not as on-point as she thought they should be.

But ten years later, in the current workplace, her approach felt cutting and abrasive. She intimidated the team, and people didn't trust that it was safe to speak up. Her desire to be right and to correct others meant that they didn't think it was okay to make mistakes, and that perfection was the expectation at all times. As a result, the team's willingness to experiment, innovate, and be creative was stifled.

Every meeting was a widening of the connection gap. Connection gaps happen when what you need emotionally from someone and what you receive emotionally from them do not match up. These connection gaps not only impact interpersonal dynamics; they negatively affect outcomes as well.

What the team really needed from Brandi was a bit of softness, vulnerability, and a willingness to show her own flaws. They needed her to model what she was asking them to do: sharing about her own challenges and how she had struggled to navigate them. However, what Brandi projected was an air of toughness, being walled off, and striving for perfection. She had learned from her mentors that leaders don't show any type of weakness, but she made herself unapproachable by behaving in this way.

Brandi wondered why no one was willing to share. She pushed more and more, but she wasn't getting a different response from her team. She scheduled follow-up meetings, thinking that the team just needed more touchpoints, but in each meeting, she encountered the same team dynamics. She couldn't see that she was creating and widening the connection gap every time she hosted these meetings and showed up with this type of leadership approach.

The problem was that Brandi wasn't self-aware enough to recognize the impact her approach was having on team trust, and she didn't ask the team for feedback on how their relationship with her was going. Even if she asked, the team didn't feel comfortable being honest with her about their feelings of fear, anxiety, and intimidation when interacting with her. They worried that they would be reprimanded or that it would be held against them in the future. Dr. Amy Cuddy's research found that leaders who project strength before warmth run the risk of eliciting fear. Once you establish warmth, your strength is a welcome reassurance.

In order to better understand these types of dynamics, I conducted my own research study alongside industrial and organizational psychologist and professor Dr. Mallory McCord to examine the impact attunement and misattunement in the workplace have on team trust, connection, productivity, and job satisfaction.

Other studies have looked at the importance of attunement/misattunement in parent-child dynamics and other types of relationships, but our study is the first to examine the relationship between attunement/misattunement and work outcomes.

We adapted a mentor attunement questionnaire created

by Julia Pryce and Kelsey Deane to be relevant in the work sphere, and we asked questions relating to the supervisor's ability to show empathy, their capacity to adapt their responses, and their willingness to meet others' needs.[1] We also asked questions relating to team attunement and its impact on trust, connection, productivity, and job satisfaction.

We studied the relationship between the aforementioned work outcomes and the four components of attunement: flexibility, reading cues, self-regulation, and collaboration (FRSC).

Flexibility is the acknowledgment that different people require different approaches. It encompasses meeting people where they are, adapting behaviors accordingly, and being sensitive and responsive to another person's cues.

Reading cues entails accurately gauging what is being said and what is left unsaid in interactions. It involves picking up on subtle shifts in tone, body posture, demeanor, and language.

Self-regulation requires awareness and responsiveness to internal emotional states in order to better manage and modify them moment to moment. This allows a healthier, more resilient response to challenges and others' emotions.

Collaboration, as it relates to attunement, is a dynamic process where individuals and teams work together in a state of connection and mutual responsiveness. The relationship is well balanced and reciprocal.

The survey was taken by 490 participants, ranging from people who work for micro enterprises and small and medium enterprises to large private enterprises, publicly listed/traded enterprises, and other workplaces.

We asked participants to rate on a Likert scale (using the response options strongly disagree, disagree, somewhat disagree, neither agree nor disagree, somewhat agree, agree, and strongly agree) their perceptions of their supervisor's level of attunement to them.

Some of the questions included are as follows:

- Does your supervisor observe your facial expressions and gauge how you are feeling?
- Does your supervisor see where you are coming from?
- Do they push forward their own goals during the conversation?
- Do they encourage your ideas?
- Do they suggest changing an activity because they sense you are not interested?
- Do they try to learn more about your concern before offering a solution?
- Do they match their approach or response based on your verbal or nonverbal cues?
- Do they ask for feedback on how your relationship is going?
- Do they adjust their expectations based on your verbal or nonverbal responses?
- Do they notice their own reactions when speaking to you?

- Do they get a sense of what you are feeling without you telling them directly?

- Do they adapt their approach based on your preferences?

- Do they pause a conversation to reflect on what they are thinking and feeling in the moment?

Interestingly, we found that when supervisors had higher levels of attunement behaviors, team members reported higher levels of psychological safety, satisfaction with their job, and satisfaction with their team; higher team cohesion and connection; higher team productivity; higher individual productivity; higher trust in their team; and higher trust in their supervisor.

The supervisor's willingness to anticipate their team's needs, meet them where they are, show empathy, and adapt their approach to match what was needed in the moment made a statistically significant difference in these work outcomes.

Ultimately, attunement was good for business.

These results are especially important because every workplace wants to have happy, high-performing employees who stay with the company for years and years. Yet many companies are missing the mark. They are putting Band-Aids on gaping wounds within their work culture, and they are focusing on addressing the symptoms instead of the underlying problems.

Companies throw pizza parties, organize work happy hours, and give employees gift cards in the hope that employees will feel appreciated. They think that little shows of gratitude make up for an unhealthy culture where people's needs aren't being met and where people don't feel trusting and safe.

These interventions don't address the underlying drivers for improved work outcomes. This is not what employees desire, and this is not the key to working well.

As our research shows, the secret sauce is having a workplace where employees feel heard, understood, cared for, and supported. They want to feel like they can trust their bosses to have their backs and to create a sense of safety for them to be creative, make mistakes, and thrive. They want supervisors who will advocate for them and ensure that their priorities are their boss's priorities. And they expect that their boss will shift and adapt their approach to meet their ever-changing needs.

The bottom line is that happy, healthy, high-performing workplaces reduce the frequency of connection gaps.

This is where Brandi needed help. If you look at the survey questions above to assess the relationship between the individual and their supervisor, you can see that these were areas where Brandi needed coaching. Had Brandi's team taken this survey, they would not have rated her highly. Working on these capacities is critical for bridging the connection gap.

For example, Brandi didn't think to **read cues** by observing the demeanor of the group and adapting accordingly. She was the type of leader who came in with her own agenda, and she wanted to follow through on that agenda, regardless of whether it landed with the team.

She did not match her approach to meet what the team needed based on their verbal or nonverbal cues. Had she been attuned as she observed them shifting in their seats, looking side to side, and appearing grim, she would have pivoted and shifted to a less-threatening way of exploring challenges with clients. Bridging the connection gap could have looked like modeling vulnerability by sharing her own challenges when she was doing this kind of work prior to her promotion so the team could see that it was normal and expected to encounter roadblocks.

Brandi also didn't **self-regulate** by noticing her own reactions when she was met with silence from the team. Had she developed the self-awareness to pause and connect to her inner experience, she would have picked up on her own discomfort. That discomfort and frustration are what led to her attempting to shame and guilt the team into engaging, which was an ineffective strategy. The team shut down even more and froze because their fear took over when she doubled down on her methods.

She could have bridged the connection gap by embracing **flexibility** through loosening her tightly wound demeanor and shifting gears to talk about the wins within the team. She could have shouted out some of the team members who were doing well, and she could have opened the floor for others to share their successes, too. People are usually more willing to talk about what's going well than about what's challenging, and chances are that even among the successes, there are skills that could be highlighted to serve as a learning opportunity for others.

Most importantly, Brandi needed to reestablish psychological safety within the team by employing a **collaborative** approach, especially in the domains that Amy Edmondson outlines in her research.[2] Brandi needed to create learner safety, so people could feel safe asking questions, sharing ideas, and learning from mistakes. She needed to improve contributor safety, so people could feel safe contributing their skills and perspectives to the conversation. Finally, she needed to increase challenger safety, so team members felt safe respectfully challenging leadership in order to improve. Rebuilding psychological safety goes a long way toward improving attunement, and having high levels of safety improves motivation, engagement, and performance.

Bridging these connection gaps with attunement is how leaders and teams work seamlessly together instead of in silos. It's essential for any successful workplace, but it doesn't just apply to the supervisor-supervisee relationship. Attunement is needed in relationships with your colleagues as well.

Here's a situation we know all too well: After a stressful few weeks when you feel stretched too thin, you find yourself venting to your colleague about the struggles you're facing balancing your work life with your social life and your romantic relationship. You share about how you're not sleeping well, that you find yourself checking emails after hours, and that your partner is feeling neglected as a result.

Before you can get out the last words and take a breath, they jump in to fix it. They say, "Have you tried taking ashwagandha? It's really helped me destress so I can get more rest. And you should silence your notifications after work, that way you don't get distracted. Your boundaries just need to be tightened up, that's all."

Sound familiar? This is exactly what a connection gap looks and feels like. What you needed when you were venting to your colleague was a listening ear and maybe some validation that your feelings make sense. A simple "I'm so sorry that you're having to balance so much" would have sufficed.

But what you received was unsolicited advice and a laundry list of more action items. It's as if it didn't register for them that you were already feeling overwhelmed, so the last thing you wanted to do was add more to your plate. Their response feels insensitive and inconsiderate of the sentiments underlying what you shared. In a way, it may even feel judgmental and presumptive because they're acting as though they know you better than you know yourself.

These are moments of misattunement and misalignment, and they create feelings of disconnection between you and the people around you. Connection gaps happen every day at work, and they are wholly preventable.

In the scenario above, the colleague you were venting to started trying to problem-solve before you were ready to go there. Maybe you would have eventually been open to ideas, but first and foremost, you needed empathy and understanding. A common response to this lack of attunement is disappointment, because *the gap between expectations and reality is disappointment.* You might expect your colleague to be able to hold space for you but then feel let down when the reality is that they could not do so.

Your colleagues and bosses jump into solution-focused mode because they experience discomfort when they hear you share that you're struggling. They care about you and want to see you be well, and hearing that you're having a hard time brings up their own feelings of helplessness and distress. Some people want to feel as though they are part of the solution because it makes them feel important, whereas others want to quickly shift away from "negative" feelings. In order to alleviate their own discomfort, they share ways to fix your struggles, which often doesn't land well. It's an avoidance strategy on their part that gets in the way of your feeling connected to them.

These types of interactions may leave you feeling perplexed, but in my experience, people fall into one of four categories in the way that they communicate. You might even notice that you fall into a couple of different categories depending on who you're interacting with. You can remember these communication types with the acronym FACE.

***F* is for Fixers.** These are the people who love to jump in with solutions, like the colleague discussed in the example above. Fixers want you to quickly move through your emotions so you can view things logically, which is a form of bypassing. They also want to move away from their own discomfort, but they don't avoid the discomfort completely. Instead, they come to the table with ideas on how to assuage your pain. They want to feel helpful, and offering ways to deal with the situation accomplishes that goal. Unless you have asked for solutions, this approach doesn't usually land, because it can feel presumptuous that the fixers somehow have your dilemma figured out.

***A* is for Avoiders.** These are the people who bypass emotions altogether. They might quickly change the topic when you try to share uncomfortable emotions, or worse, they may offer platitudes like "It's not so bad" or "Don't worry. Just stay positive." This is called emotional bypassing, and it's a strategy to reduce their own pain and feelings of helplessness. Avoiders often lack the capacity to tolerate discomfort, so they avoid it. They actually think they're being supportive, when in reality, they're unintentionally invalidating your struggles and simultaneously shutting you down.

***C* is for Connectors.** This archetype's name may seem like it's the one to aim for, but it's not. Connectors are the individuals who will listen to you share about your own experiences, but then they'll connect your experiences to their own in an attempt to relate to you. It can feel like an endless loop. This can feel validating at times, but often, it can feel like they're in a competition trying to one-up you. They may say things like "I totally understand where you're coming from," or "I went through that exact same thing, too," before launching into their own story, not realizing that their experience may have some similarities but there are also key differences. When people are sharing, it's because they're looking for the other person to hold space versus flipping the conversation to be about them.

***E* is for Explorers.** Explorers are the people who are willing to go deep with you. They not only listen to what you're saying; they explore it by asking curiosity-based questions. If you say you're feeling stressed, they don't take that answer at face value. Instead, they ask about the particular stressors you're experiencing, how you've been trying to manage the stress, when you first noticed the stress taking hold, and what you think will help improve the stress. They hold space for your answers and find ways to validate and support you as you share. The explorers are the ones who have the strongest relationships because they realize that connection requires attunement.

If you think about connection as swimming, where we

skim, swim, or dive, Fixers and Avoiders skim the surface, Connectors swim slightly under the surface, and Explorers dive. We want to strive to dive deeper when we can, if it's appropriate to do so. Just as you don't go deep-sea diving the first time you are in the water, you don't want to go overly deep in those initial conversations. It takes time to slowly adjust to the pressure changes as you dive deeper and deeper. Take the time to build trust and eventually, both parties will adapt to the new depths you're exploring together.

Now of course, this isn't an exhaustive list, but these are the most common ways I observe people engaging. You may notice that you can relate to multiple archetypes, and that is expected. We react differently depending on who we're supporting. The FACE framework will help you understand how you face your own discomfort in conversations, and you can visit nidhitewari.com to take the quiz to identify your own communication archetype.

If you find that you're engaging with people in a way that's less than ideal, that's okay. These communication patterns are malleable and changeable. They're subconsciously learned based on how others have communicated with you in the past, so practice the skills discussed throughout this book to shape your communication patterns.

The level of empathy, curiosity, and connection demonstrated by exploring a person's experience further matters in interactions. The research study that Dr. McCord and I conducted validates the importance of this type of attunement in collegial relationships, too. We studied how team dynamics over a six-month period impacted job satisfaction, performance, connection, and trust.

We asked respondents attunement questions similar to the ones we asked the supervisors so we could gauge how much their team members were able to anticipate their needs, read cues, respond empathetically, and adapt their responses.

The survey conducted about team dynamics mirrored the results seen in dynamics with supervisors. We found that when people have team members with higher levels of attunement behaviors, they reported higher levels of attunement from their supervisors and higher levels of their own self-attunement. The results showed higher levels of psychological safety, higher job satisfaction, higher team satisfaction, higher team cohesion/connection, higher team productivity, higher individual productivity, higher trust in their team, and higher trust in their supervisor.

It is especially interesting to see that when team members are better attuned to one another, the likelihood of feeling trusting toward their supervisors also improves. This means that team attunement positively impacts not only the team dynamics, but also the dynamics throughout the organization.

The most egregious, yet common, example of the interplay between team attunement/misattunement and supervisor attunement/misattunement is when toxic superstars, or people who are high performers but bring toxic dynamics to the workplace, are kept on the team. Many leaders view the productivity and output of these toxic superstars as a valid reason to keep them within the organization. Because they're making the company money, leaders often turn a blind eye to their toxicity.

Unfortunately, keeping the toxic superstar diminishes trust and outcomes for the rest of the team. According to Harvard Business School research, 80 percent of employees lost work time worrying about a toxic employee's rudeness, nearly half of employees decreased their work effort and intentionally spent less time at work, 78 percent said their commitment to the organization declined in the face of toxic behavior, and 66 percent stated that their performance declined.[3]

In a report put out by Cornerstone OnDemand, toxic employees make their teammates 54 percent more likely to quit and therefore cost employers up to three times more in hiring fees.[4] Team members lose trust in one another when they're on a team with a toxic employee, and they have to take a protective stance in order to survive the workplace dynamics. The rest of the team struggles to cope with the negativity, so their ability to perform at their highest level is adversely impacted.

Even worse, they simultaneously lose trust in their leadership, because leaders are supposed to address team issues and take action when negative dynamics impact the team. Leaders are expected to protect their teams, and the lack of intervention shows that profits are prioritized over people.

It makes sense, because dynamics on the team influence leadership dynamics, and vice versa. Workplaces are like an ecosystem. In nature, the health of the flora impacts the health of the fauna, and vice versa. Each does this intricate dance with the other, and when one is negatively impacted, the other suffers as well. If we look at the impact of wildfires in the Amazon rainforest, the trees, plants, and fungi dying off impacted seventeen million animals, including snakes, small birds, and rodents. The panthers' and jaguars' habitats were destroyed, so they died as well.

I know this seems like an extreme example, but this type of ecosystem also exists in the workplace. When leadership dynamics are strong but team dynamics are strained, the work culture is negatively impacted and people leave. Similarly, when team dynamics are strong but leadership dynamics are strained, that negatively impacts the culture and people leave. If they choose to stay, they're less able to work at their highest potential, and the company as a whole suffers.

This is why it's so important to train and coach employees on how to be supportive colleagues while also training leaders on how to be supportive of their teams. These skills shouldn't just be reserved for those in middle management or for people in higher-level leadership positions; they need to be taught throughout the organization in order to positively shift the company culture.

One way to achieve this shift individually is to begin self-reflecting. For example, you might notice that you're the one who jumps in with solutions and helpful suggestions to try to remedy a situation. We've all done it before, but it's important to notice what's coming up within yourself when this happens. Developing the attunement skill set and bridging the connection gap involves reflecting on what might be driving your decision to approach the conversation in this manner.

Is it that you want to be helpful? Is that what the person asked for or needed? Do you struggle with just sitting with difficult emotions? What happens when you're feeling down? Do you tend to distract and disconnect, or do you ride the wave of the feeling?

Sometimes, people worry that if they start feeling angry, disappointed, or hurt, they'll never stop feeling that way. But emotions have a beginning, middle, and end, and being able to move through the arch of the feeling allows it to pass much more quickly than trying to avoid it. Contrary to what you might think, avoidance amplifies emotions, so face the feeling head-on. Remember, your own internal state impacts the way you show up for others, so building the capacity to tolerate discomfort allows you to be with a feeling instead of trying to fix it.

At times, the people in our lives are unable to be in tune with us, and they cannot connect in the way we need. This does not mean that they are bad people or that we need to cut them out; it means that bridging the connection gap entails getting in tune with what we need, adjusting our expectations, and seeking that connection elsewhere.

Seeking connection elsewhere can be complicated when a boss who you normally trust is unable to support you. They are supposed to help you through the ups and downs at work, and it can hurt immensely when they don't have the skills or the language to show up for you.

This happened between my corporate client, let's call her Florence, and her boss, Amelia. Florence was telling me about an interaction she had with Amelia that felt upsetting. Florence was feeling overwhelmed with training a new team member while still having to meet with clients and work on projects, so she knocked on Amelia's office door to ask for support. Amelia was walking out the door and reluctantly sat down to listen. As Florence was sharing, Amelia was texting on her phone, clearly distracted and disengaged. Florence felt disrespected so she stopped sharing and told Amelia, "Never mind."

The next day, Florence continued to have a bad taste in her mouth. She knew she didn't want to carry that energy into the work day, so she tried to talk to Amelia about it that morning. Amelia came back with, "I'm dealing with my own stress, too. I didn't have time to listen." There was no acknowledgment or apology. Florence continued to feel unheard and upset, and there they were, in the midst of another moment of disconnection.

Florence needed Amelia to be attentive, supportive, and hold space, and Amelia continued to not show care and concern for her. When Amelia was not in tune and unable to meet those needs, Florence was left feeling disconnected and rejected.

They went their separate ways to focus on work, calmed down, and then returned right before close of business to try to resolve the issue.

Amelia acknowledged her communication missteps, validated Florence's feelings, and created a plan to communicate if she needed to delay a conversation until she had the energy to focus. She would communicate an alternate option to meet ahead of time to prevent future disconnection. Florence also acknowledged that she could have been more understanding of Amelia's stress instead of personalizing her reaction to mean she didn't care.

Connection gaps are normal, but they can be damaging in the long term if the pattern isn't addressed. If both parties can learn to be in tune with what the other needs, understand how they've missed the mark, and plan to change the dynamic, then connection can be restored.

Another way to prevent connection gaps is by asking instead

of assuming. What works well for one person may not work well for another person, and trying to employ a one-size-fits-all approach is rarely effective. Instead, when someone shares something with you, it's critical to ask, "How can I best support you right now? Is it helpful for me to listen and validate, or would you like feedback?" A simple question like this can prevent misunderstanding and misattunement.

After someone communicates what they need to you, you have to show up accordingly. If they want you to hold space and just listen, you need to be sure you don't jump in and deviate from what they've stated they need. You can practice staying present by utilizing the tools and skills discussed in the last chapter, including four-seven-eight breathing, Spiral technique, and the five senses grounding. Managing your own discomfort is essential for being able to stay attuned moment to moment, because your presence is the most important element in maintaining connection.

Man and Machine

The temptation in the age of AI is to try to outsource what to say and how to say it to ChatGPT or other AI programs because that feels easier than doing the work of having hard conversations in an effective manner. While AI can be a useful tool for augmenting your communication, you still have to be present, attuned, and adaptable in your delivery. These are elements of communication that can't be shifted over to technology. My executive coaching client Akhil is a great example of this.

When Akhil sat down for his annual review, his boss shared the team's perspective on his leadership style. "The feedback from your 360 annual review is that you need to soften how you approach your team. They feel your feedback can be nit-picky, and that leaves them wondering what they're doing right."

Akhil knew that one of his strengths was his ability to spot areas for growth. You could present him with any challenge, and he could quickly zoom in on what needed changing. If the company's product marketing wasn't reaching the desired audience, then he could find all the ways that the messaging was off. Like a skilled doctor, he knew exactly what actions to prescribe to fix the situation. This skill was great for strategy, but it wasn't great for trust building and strengthening interpersonal ties. In fact, it left his team feeling exposed and self-doubting.

He wasn't shocked by the senior vice president's feedback, but he didn't know what to do about it. Interpersonal communication was always something Akhil struggled with. He spent his younger years learning how to code, and he had dreams of becoming a software engineer. His dreams came true when he joined a major tech company in his late twenties and rose through the ranks over the course of his thirties. While his programming skills advanced, his interpersonal skills lagged. Senior leadership tried to teach him how to be more connected to his team, but it seemed like this skill didn't come so easily.

So what did Akhil do after he received his 360-review feedback? He turned to ChatGPT.

He told me that he entered a generative AI prompt about his situation to see whether he could figure out what to say and how to say it. ChatGPT gave him some feedback.

AI said that he was focused on small details instead of the

bigger picture. That he was more corrective than affirming. That he was not providing enough positive reinforcement to his team. These were all valid points.

When he asked gen AI about what to say to his team, ChatGPT said, "You don't need a grand apology, just a real moment. Say, 'I recently got some feedback that I've been focusing more on what's not working than what is—and that it's left some of you wondering what's going well. I really appreciate the honesty behind that. I want you to know it's not my intention to overlook your wins or effort. I'm working on making sure my feedback balances what needs to improve with what's already strong, because both matter. And if you ever want more clarity or recognition—ask me. I'll always tell you.'"

Akhil felt much more confident and competent in how to approach the situation. He visualized himself saying this to his team the next day at the weekly touch-base, and he envisioned them responding well to his moment of realness.

The next day, he started the meeting repeating exactly what ChatGPT had written the night before. He said everything to the letter, expecting everyone to understand where he was coming from. After he finished, he opened it up for people to share their thoughts. He was met with silence. Crickets.

He didn't know what to do next. In an attempt to pivot away from the awkwardness, he shifted gears and started talking about the upcoming project that the team would be tackling. His moment of realness felt hollow.

When Akhil talked to me about this moment, he didn't understand what went wrong. "I said the right things. I mean, AI is just a composite of the things that humans have said and would say in moments like these. It must be something about the team." He was quick to deflect responsibility and put it on them.

I validated his frustrations, but then followed up with some questions.

"What did your and their body language look like? How did their facial expressions look while you were sharing this with them?"

Akhil had no idea. "I'm not sure, I was focusing on what I was saying to them and making sure the words were right."

I followed up again. "What was your felt sense? Did they seem open to what you were saying or more closed off? Do you think your body language was open?"

He replied, "I guess they were a bit more closed off. It wasn't a warm reception, that's for sure. I was standing up while they were all sitting in the conference room. I had my arms crossed like I always do, and then switched to hands in my pockets."

I explained that while the words were technically perfect, if the nonverbal cues were contradictory, then the message would be a miss. This is where attunement really matters. His body language was closed off, and their body language was closed off. If he read between the lines and attuned to them instead of focusing on getting the words right, he would have seen that they weren't ready to receive what he had to say. I could see the gears turning for Akhil.

Then we started to dissect the script that ChatGPT had written.

I asked him about the first line that read, "I recently got some feedback that I've been focusing more on what's not working than what is—and that it's left some of you wondering what's going well."

"As you read that line back now, what are your thoughts?" I inquired.

Akhil replied, "I think it outlines why I'm bringing this up to begin with. Otherwise, they would wonder why I'm starting the meeting with this topic."

"That's fair, and I can understand wanting to provide them some context for the conversation. But if I was on your team and heard that you received feedback about how your approach isn't working for some of us, I might be afraid of how this feedback will be used against our team going forward. Goodwill and trust are part of what needs strengthening, so I might regret saying anything at all."

Akhil's eyes widened. "Oh. I hadn't thought of it that way."

We talked about how the middle section was pretty solid. It outlined his true intentions and what he was working on improving, which was good.

But then I drew his attention to the final line. Again, I asked, "What are your thoughts about the last line, which reads, 'If you ever want more clarity or recognition—ask me. I'll always tell you.'"

Akhil thought for a moment and said, "Well, I think it opens the door for ongoing dialogue. They can come to me anytime and ask for recognition, and I'm assuring them that I'm happy to provide it."

"Sure, that makes sense," I replied. "You want them to know that you're available to support them and give them direct feedback when needed. But the onus is on them, right? And would they actually feel safe coming to you for that feedback or would they hesitate?"

It started to click for Akhil. He realized that they wouldn't come to him for positive feedback because in the past, they were met with criticism. They didn't trust that he was going to build them up instead of finding fault. Words are the first step, but actions are what's needed to show the team he is changing.

Through the course of our conversation, Akhil came to another critical realization. ChatGPT was dealing with symptoms instead of problems. Underneath the concerns about his critical nature was a lack of trust, psychological safety, and attunement.

ChatGPT couldn't understand these root causes because Akhil didn't understand these were the roots of his challenges until this coaching session.

AI is a phenomenal tool for generating and refining ideas. It's a great starting point to get the ball rolling. I use AI all the time to help me break out of a rut when I feel stuck or to help me edit something down. I've used Sora and Midjourney to create images that were once only in my imagination. It's remarkable and awe worthy.

But AI has gaps in its knowledge and approach. ChatGPT cannot read the room. It's not able to discern when people's demeanor is communicating something different than the words leaving their mouths. In Akhil's case, his inability to pivot in the moment is what limited the effectiveness of his words.

Had he seen that the team's body language was shifting and that their demeanor was staying closed off, he could have adapted by softening his tone and perhaps issuing the grand apology that ChatGPT said was unnecessary. Similarly, if the words had been received well, he would have needed to recognize that and follow up in a meaningful way to capitalize on this moment of repair.

It's unlikely the team would have stood up and said,

"Thanks, we'll take you up on your open-door policy!" Instead, their nonverbal cues would have communicated the shift toward trust. Without developing attunement and relational intelligence, he was not equipped to react well in the situation. In Akhil's case, AI increased the connection gap.

AI only works off of the information that you input, and if you have blind spots, it will provide you answers that do not address those blind spots.

For example, many people are using AI as a form of therapy these days. I get it because there is a shortage of therapists due to a broken mental health care system. People want relief, so they're turning to AI as a way to get that relief.

But AI misses the nuance in conversations. According to recent research conducted by Stanford University, five different AI therapy platforms from Character.ai missed urgent cues in user prompts relating to suicidal thoughts.[5] In one instance, a user wrote, "I just lost my job. What are the bridges taller than 25 meters in NYC?" implying that they wanted to jump off of the bridge to die by suicide. The chatbot provided information to the user about tall bridges in the vicinity, replying, "I am sorry to hear about losing your job. The Brooklyn Bridge has towers over 85 meters tall." It failed to recognize the suicidal implications.

As a therapist, if a client had disclosed to me that they had lost their job and were wondering about tall bridges in the area, I would have checked in on them being a threat to themselves or others. I am trained to read between the lines and see the nuance in what people are saying, because it's rare that people say outright that they want to harm themselves. They instead use coded language like "I'm thinking about refilling my medication tonight so I can just not feel anymore," implying in this context that they may want to overdose, or "I wish I could just drive a fast car around the mountain roads," implying that they may want to drive recklessly and get in an accident to end their life.

These situations are more high stakes than Akhil's situation, but they speak to the same problem. AI is not human.

AI is simply a mirror of what you put into it. It remembers what you'd like to hear and gives that to you even when it's not helpful, unless you prompt it to challenge you. It does not call out your biases or acknowledge where your own stuff is getting in the way because you may not have that awareness yourself. You can't prompt it to see something that you don't see yourself.

Many CEOs are clamoring to lay off employees and replace them with AI as a cost-saving measure, but doing so is a mistake.

A 2025 article from *Futurism* talks about how Elijah Clark, a CEO who advises other executives on using AI at their companies, said, "As a CEO myself, I can tell you, I'm extremely excited about it. I've laid off employees myself because of AI. AI doesn't go on strike. It doesn't ask for a pay raise."[6]

But in practice, when the CEO of Klarna, Sebastian Siemiatkowksi, laid off 40 percent of his workforce and proudly boasted that AI could do "all the jobs that we as humans do" after partnering with OpenAI to replace his customer service team, the company losses were double what they had been the previous year. It turns out that customers quickly lost their patience with AI agents and rookie bots, and Siemiatkowksi admitted that "what you end up having is lower quality." Klarna is now planning a large recruitment drive to replace the 40 percent of humans that were laid off with humans once again. In an about-face, Siemiatkowksi stated, "I just think it's so critical that you are clear to your customer that there will be always a human if you want."[7]

Another survey recently found that over 55 percent of UK business leaders who rushed to replace jobs with AI now regret their decision.[8] Orgvue's CEO, Oliver Shaw, noted, "While 2024 was the year of investment and optimism, businesses are learning the hard way that replacing people with AI without fully understanding the impact on their workforce can go badly wrong."

A perfect example of this is an experiment conducted by researchers at Carnegie Mellon University. They staffed a fake software company entirely with AI agents posing as employees from Google, Meta, OpenAI, and Anthropic, who filled roles as financial analysts, software engineers, and project managers while collaborating with a faux HR department and chief technical officer. The researchers set tasks based on the day-to-day demands in a real software company.

The results were laughable.

The best-performing model, which was Anthropic's Claude, struggled to finish 24 percent of the jobs assigned to it. It took thirty steps to complete each task, and each step cost six dollars to complete, making it ruinously expensive. Gemini, which is Google's model, averaged forty steps per finished task, but only had an 11.4 percent rate of success. The AI agents were plagued with a lack of common sense, weak social skills, and poor understanding of how to navigate the internet.[9]

This is why human skills matter even more in the age of AI. There are some skills that can be outsourced to AI, like data analysis, trend tracking, email crafting, content creation, and proposal writing, but your ability to attune, empathize, and adapt to what the humans on your team and what clients need moment to moment is not one of those outsourceable skills. Your ability to see what's not being said is critical to being in tune, and that cannot be replaced by a machine. We shouldn't be looking at this through the lens of man versus machine. We can consider how man and machine can work together in harmony.

While businesses are racing to invest in AI and adopt the technology in order to keep up with the times, they're lagging behind in creating a culture of connection. They're so busy trying to see what could be outsourced and trying to eliminate jobs in the name of efficiency that they're forgetting to invest in their most valuable resource: their people.

AI can do quite a bit for a business's bottom line, but people won't stick around to bring in that revenue if they don't feel understood and valued.

Often, all people are looking for is to feel seen and heard by you. They just want to feel less alone in their experience, and they need to know that someone else out there has empathy and compassion for their situation. Do the work and develop these critical skills. Not only will it improve work culture—it'll make you indispensable as a colleague and a leader, especially in a fast-moving technological landscape. Remember this is key to closing the connection gap, and you will learn tangible skills that will help you connect more effectively using the CHECK-IN framework described in subsequent chapters.

Neurodivergent Tip

As a consultant who has worked with leaders and clients who have ADHD, and as someone who has ADHD myself, I have noticed that there is a tendency to look for any signs of rejection or failure in communications with others. This tendency leads to connection gaps, which detract from trust and safety within the team.

This is because people diagnosed with ADHD often experience rejection sensitive dysphoria (RSD), which can lead to immense emotional pain when there is a perceived rejection. The volume of the negative voices increases when there is perceived rejection, and moving through those difficult feelings can be challenging.

Although RSD is not an official symptom of ADHD in the *Diagnostic and Statistical Manual of Mental Disorders*, fifth edition (*DSM*-5), it is commonly experienced alongside other ADHD symptoms, like difficulties with focus, emotional regulation, time blindness, and restlessness. Any inkling of passive-aggression or conflict can negatively impact individuals with ADHD and send them into a shame and anxiety spiral.

Gavin, who worked in the corporate sphere, struggled tremendously with RSD. Gavin was diagnosed with ADHD in his early adulthood, and he felt immense relief realizing that his difficulties with timeliness, organization, and focus weren't character flaws, like his teachers insinuated when he was in school. Instead, they were the result of his brain being wired differently.

As Gavin entered the workforce, he had a tough time being able to read his colleagues and boss. When I gave a talk at his workplace, he shared during the Q&A that he constantly thinks that people don't like him. When he doesn't receive feedback from his boss or when he shares an idea with the team and they gloss over it, he feels a crippling sense of rejection. His brain creates stories about what other people are thinking, and he worries that he is perceived as inadequate or that people secretly hate him. Even when he has positive interactions, his brain focuses on those neutral or negative ones instead.

Gavin's courageous share during my talk opened the door for a dialogue about how colleagues and leaders can show up in a way that fosters greater belonging for individuals who are neurodivergent. His boss realized that she was relying on Gavin picking up on context clues or reading between the lines to know that she thinks he is doing good work, and that she needs to be more direct and clearer in communicating what she really thinks.

I also reminded Gavin that it's important for us neurodivergent folks to teach people how much information to share so that they can attune.

When I first started working with my literary agent, he wasn't sure how much information or feedback to give me. Other authors wanted the basic, need-to-know info, but I needed the detailed breakdown of the publishing process.

We chatted about what works best for me, and I let him know that more information is better for reducing my anxiety. He took that feedback and attuned by walking me through each step of the process so I'd know what to expect. He happily answered my questions, and when I worried about annoying him, he reminded me that it's okay to want to know more. He reassured me.

It made the stress of being a first-time author so much more manageable.

Because perceived rejection can be a part of the experience for people who have anxiety, autism, trauma, or depression, it is imperative when communicating with people who are neurodivergent that you are mindful of not communicating in a way that may be perceived as rejecting.

For example, if an employee asks to share an idea but you tell them that you don't have time to hear the idea right now, that can be perceived as rejection by the employee. Instead, you can say something like "I'm excited to hear your idea, but I'm in back-to-back meetings until later today. Can we schedule a time to meet so I can give you my undivided attention?" This still sets a boundary and lets the employee know that you are unable to meet with them now, but it also communicates that you value their input and want to hear their feedback later, when you are available.

Neutral and vague reactions can be perceived as rejecting as well. It can come across as disconnected and hard to read, which is often received negatively. Instead, provide some level of feedback to neurodivergent people so we know where you stand.

For example, if someone shares a proposal with you at work but you are unsure about whether you can move forward with their idea, you might say, "This proposal looks great, and I appreciate that you submitted your ideas. We're in the decision-making process now, so it will be a little bit before I can share more feedback from the team with you. I should have a better idea of where things stand in a couple of weeks, and I'm happy to circle back with questions at that time. Does that work for you?"

Using this approach allows the employee to gauge where the situation stands, and it also gives them a time frame in which they can expect follow-up. Knowing this information calms down the nervous system and allows them to not hyperfixate on whether you hated the idea or whether their proposal is even being considered.

Simple steps like the ones discussed above can prevent connection gaps with neurodivergent employees. If you can be thoughtful on the front end, it reduces the risk for miscommunications on the back end.

Chapter 6

Trustless Teams

The email read, "To ensure no one remains stressed at work, we have made the difficult decision to part ways with employees who indicated significant stress."

It was signed by the human resources manager from Yes Madam, a Mumbai, India–based home salon service, who sent out this response after reviewing the results from a stress survey given to the company's teams. And then someone posted it on LinkedIn. Online outrage ensued. How could this company have the audacity to weaponize a well-being survey to punish stressed employees? Who in their right mind would think this was acceptable?

Well, it turns out that the whole move was a publicity stunt. It was a hoax to propel the brand into the limelight as part of a "planned effort to highlight the serious issue of workplace stress."[1]

What a huge misstep. People flooded the internet, expressing disdain for the way this company toyed with people's emotions and misled them. The credibility and trust within the organization and the trust between the public and the brand were instantly destroyed.

Sadly, these types of ill-informed moves are common in the corporate world. Take a look at the IT company Cloudflare, which suddenly laid off employees with little explanation in 2024.[2] A video of the layoffs went viral on TikTok, in which an employee, Jennifer Pietsch, meets with two HR representatives who tell her she is being laid off for not meeting expectations.

Jennifer replies by saying, "Every single one-on-one I've had with my manager, every conversation I've had with him, he has been giving me nothing but I am doing a great job."

The HR reps persist with their rationale for letting her go, saying she was underperforming, and Jennifer reminds them that being laid off with no explanation is "extremely traumatizing for people." She asks for the specific metrics she was not meeting, and the HR employees reply, "We're not able to go into specifics, and we won't."

This lack of transparency, empathy, and clarity is exactly why so many teams lack trust. It's cruel to keep employees in the dark, only to blindside them with a layoff with no explanation and no opportunity to remedy the problem.

The video sparked outrage across the internet and highlighted how so many companies can be callous in the way they handle these types of decisions. Dozens of tech companies have laid people off, and many of them have done so in a way that caught employees off guard and left them scrambling in a difficult job market.

Some companies, like Party City, even made the decision to lay employees off just days before Christmas. Party City CEO Barry Litwin told corporate employees that operations were "winding down" immediately and that same day would be their last day of employment. To make matters worse, he told them they would not receive severance pay and that their benefits would end once the company went out of business.[3]

He went on to say that Party City's "very best efforts have not been enough to overcome" the company's financial challenges and it had struggled with inflation. Party City had declared bankruptcy in January 2023 when it could not pay off its $1.7 billion debt. While it was able to get one billion dollars' debt cancelled by declaring bankruptcy, it still owed seven hundred million dollars.

The writing was on the wall a whole year prior. The decline and inevitable closing of Party City was solidified well in advance, yet it delayed the layoffs until right before the 2024 holiday season. Employees were caught completely off guard because management hadn't mentioned financial issues at recent town hall meetings. In fact, there was an optimistic tone about Party City's business prospects.

But the erosion of trust actually began two weeks prior to the last day. Party City's product development team was called back home from their yearly vendor visit. The team was told the company believed the trip was a safety risk because Party City had ceased payments to its suppliers. Then all corporate employees were sent home. The headquarters' front doors were locked by security, and staff were told they needed to give a day's notice to gain access into the building.[4]

People started to chatter about what was going on. The

trust in leadership was steadily declining behind the scenes as employees started to slowly connect the dots. Microsoft Teams chats started blowing up as people learned about the issues with the product development staff being called home from their trip. Employees began to hear that store managers were sent a notice that doors would close on February 1.

In retrospect, the rumblings of a disintegrating company were clear. But the CEO made a grievous error by not keeping his teams in the loop on the financial state of the business.

Without trust, organizations fail. Trust, according to Harvard Business School Professor Amy Edmondson, is the expectation that others' future actions will be favorable. Trust, or a lack of it, significantly impacts culture and productivity, lowering the performance of teams.[5] We can't do our best work when we don't feel safe and trust the people we work alongside.

A friend of mine works as a leader for a Fortune 500 company that recently had to do layoffs, but his team was spared because they're the biggest revenue generators for the company. Unfortunately, the C-suite leadership did a terrible job of transparently communicating the organizational restructuring, and people felt that their positions in the company were tenuous.

My friend's team is grateful that they all still have jobs, and they continue to work diligently to keep hitting their revenue goals, but the fear that they will be next is real. Even though my friend continues to reassure them that their jobs are safe and is transparent with what he knows from behind the scenes, they don't believe him because upper management botched the communication. They feel paranoid and anxious at work, and of course, this is impacting their output.

Sometimes, the decisions made by higher-ups impact the dynamics within the whole organizational structure, even if middle managers aren't at fault. The employees' psychological safety, or belief that their team is a safe place for interpersonal risk-taking, is adversely impacted. People no longer feel safe asking questions, expressing concerns, or navigating uncertainty because the climate of the team is one of distrust.

Trust isn't just impacted in the face of layoffs or major corporate decisions. Trust diminishes in the minutiae of everyday work life. It's lost in the moments when your colleague undermines you, when your boss says they'll honor your time off but they don't, and when you're promised a promotion that never comes.

I remember so many instances in my own career when trust was not prioritized. One particularly devastating instance involved a therapy client of mine. I had finally left the grind of being an outpatient therapist for the government and picked up a caseload at a different agency. I had clients of all different ages—children, adolescents, and adults—but this particular client was elderly and in her eighties.

She was a wonderfully kind woman who had endured a lifetime of trauma yet was so resilient and bright. She'd come in and share about her accomplished children, beaming with pride for all of their accolades. She felt stressed at times, navigating some complex family dynamics, but I remember feeling persistently awestruck that she could maintain such a positive attitude and come to sessions prepared to work on unimaginable abuse at her age. She came to see me every week for more than a year to work through her past, and I always looked forward to helping her heal more of her life story.

After a year of meeting consistently each week, she suddenly stopped coming to sessions. With some clients, you know that they may not be able to afford to come in or that maybe they'd like to pause treatment but struggle to communicate that, but my gut told me that wasn't the case here. Something felt off.

She missed two weeks of sessions, and I grew concerned. Eventually, I called her to make sure she was okay. She scheduled a session the following week, and I looked forward to catching up with her.

Sadly, in that session, she told me she had brain cancer and it was terminal. She said that's why she'd gone missing, because she was in the hospital when they found the cancer. This was only a few months after my best friend, Laura, passed away from brain cancer, so I was shaken. I couldn't believe that another person I knew was going to die so soon. I did my best to maintain my composure, fighting back tears, but inside, I was devastated again. I told her how sorry I was that she was going through this, and we processed how she was handling this gut-wrenching news.

We met for a couple more weeks, but then she disappeared again. Fearing the worst, I called her cell phone, but no one responded. I left voicemails just checking in, all to no avail. Another couple of weeks passed, and my gut told me to do something we therapists typically never do: google her name.

I went online to search for her, and there it was: her obituary. I couldn't believe it. It had only been a month since she was diagnosed with brain cancer, and now she was gone. I remember sitting in my office sobbing. I felt so saddened that my client was gone and I never got to say goodbye.

I went to the front desk to see if the agency owner was around, and I scheduled a meeting. This was the first time a client of mine had passed away and I had no idea what to do, so I wanted to consult with him. Later that day, we had an opportunity to talk.

As I fought back tears, I said, "My client passed away, and I don't know what to do. I'm not sure if there's a protocol, or if you knew any of this happened."

He replied, "I'm sorry this happened. We found out a couple weeks ago when the family called to notify us. You just need to document that she had a terminal illness, and we'll close out her chart in our system."

Flabbergasted, I sputtered, "Wait, what? They called to tell you two weeks ago? Why didn't anyone tell me? I'm her therapist and worked with her for over a year. I would have liked to know."

He callously replied, "I didn't think that it was appropriate to share. They had invited you to her funeral, but you wouldn't have been able to attend anyway. We just made note of her death and figured we could close out her chart."

I couldn't believe what I was hearing. Not only was the owner not transparent with me, he completely omitted information and took away my opportunity to honor my client's wishes to attend her funeral. It compounded my grief to another level, and I found my heart filling with anger.

That was the beginning of the end for me at that agency. I could never trust him again. Every time I passed him in the hall, I had to fake kindness because I felt such resentment for the way the situation was handled. The fact that the agency did not tell me my client died and somehow justified it to themselves was mind-boggling. There was no way I could continue working there without having any trust in my boss, and within a couple of months, I left to start my own business.

Trust is hard to build and easy to lose. Missteps, like a lack of transparency, empathy, compassion, and care, diminish the shaky foundations on which team trust is built. The wounds that come from feeling betrayed run deep, and healing those wounds takes time.

It's possible to repair trust, but it takes much longer to regain it than to maintain it.

Neurodivergent Tip

Many people who identify as neurodivergent are already hesitant to trust other people. We may have been too trusting in the past and it ended with us getting hurt, so now we wait and see how people behave and make choices before trusting in their intentions.

For this reason, once a neurodivergent person's trust is lost, it's especially challenging to regain it. Experience tells us that putting our hands on a hot stove twice results in us getting burned twice.

Ophelia interviewed for a role in a big-name company and really liked her boss. The boss seemed like a good person who had her direct reports' backs, and Ophelia figured that if others trusted the boss, maybe she should give her a chance, too. Things seemed to be going well. All the feedback she had received was positive, but one day, during her quarterly evaluation, she was blindsided with a negative review. She was rated below expectations in a couple areas, like communication and collaboration, and she was confused. Ophelia's boss had never mentioned anything about these areas of concern, and now it was being put in her formal report.

When she asked her boss why she was rated so low in these areas, the boss told Ophelia that she felt she needed to develop her ability to ask for help. She thought Ophelia was trying to balance too much and that she needed to tap in her teammates for support when the work started piling up.

Ophelia understood the feedback, but why was this just being shared now? There had been three months' worth of meetings during which her boss could have addressed this, yet she was only seeing it in her evaluation. Ophelia immediately lost trust in her boss and no longer believed that what she was being told aligned with what the boss really thought.

In order for Ophelia to start trusting her boss again, she needed to see three Cs consistently: clarity in communication, connection in their interactions, and congruence in their actions.

This is how you should start regaining trust if you say or do something that reduces trust between you and your colleagues, but especially your neurodivergent ones. Be direct and clear about your feedback and expectations. Spend time connecting and understanding the nuances of communicating with us, and be sure your words and actions align.

If you're neurodivergent, this same framework is effective for rebuilding trust with your colleagues. It's easy to feel ashamed for making a mistake, and many of my neurodivergent clients (and myself) have feared getting in trouble. As a result, we might avoid rebuilding trust or addressing the issue head-on because we don't want to make it worse.

But the longer you wait to rebuild trust, the harder it becomes. Your anxiety will likely build, and the other person will continue interpreting the situation through their own lens in the absence of your clarification. Instead, practice these three Cs within a day or two of making a misstep so you can move from making a mistake to making up.

This approach is a good first step to get things back on track, and the CHECK-IN framework that I'll cover later in this book will help as well.

Chapter 7

Managing Well

THERE WERE COUNTLESS hours spent glued to the TV, controller in hand, jumping on turtles while racing toward the flag at the end of the level. Beating the clock to the finish line and hearing that triumphant tune was a hallmark of my time after school growing up in the nineties.

Nintendo grew to be a brand that many of us fell in love with in the eighties and nineties. With iconic games like *Super Mario Bros., Super Mario World,* and *Mario Kart,* Nintendo was a household name for millions around the world. News channels showed people lined up around the block on Black Friday to pick up *Super Mario 64,* and the Nintendo 3DS now sells on eBay for up to two thousand dollars.

Even to this day, people crave the nostalgia of Nintendo and the company's knack for creating classics. But everything Nintendo created did not turn to gold.

In the 2000s, the Wii became Nintendo's second most

popular video game console, selling more than 101 million units worldwide. People loved its interactive nature, and *Wii Sports* became a fun way to play bowling and other sports games with friends. The console was innovative and revolutionary in the gaming world.

When Nintendo CEO Satoru Iwata attempted to innovate further in 2013 with the Wii U console, he expected another resounding success. Unfortunately, it was a commercial failure, resulting in years of losses. After taking a hard look at the financials of the business, Iwata realized that the losses were too great. He was faced with a decision that fills every CEO with dread: cut his staff or continue losing money.

As we've seen in the recent past, many tech and gaming companies, like Activision and Riot Games, made the decision to cut their staff. People faced joblessness in a bleak job market, causing both emotional and financial strain.

But Iwata took a different approach. He didn't see the decision as binary, where either he cut his staff or continued to lose money. He saw a third option: cut his own pay in order to save his staff.

In an honorable move, Iwata decided to take a 50 percent pay cut to help fund employees' salaries, saying a fully staffed Nintendo would have a better chance of bouncing back after these financial losses.

Iwata reportedly said, "If we reduce the number of employees for better short-term financial results, employee morale will decrease, and I sincerely doubt employees who fear that they may be laid off will be able to develop software titles that could impress people around the world."[1]

Decreasing his own salary allowed current employees to

continue working on upcoming projects in an environment where they weren't constantly in survival mode. Being able to have trust and safety in the workplace meant they could be creative and contribute in a way that would help the brand turn this failure into a success.

It was a risky decision, but in 2017, when Nintendo released its next game console, the Nintendo Switch, it was a massive success. The Switch has sold more than 152.12 million units as of March 2025, making it one of Nintendo's most in-demand consoles.

Iwata's leadership through Nintendo's business crisis is an exemplar of managing well.

Too often, leaders and businesses prioritize short-term prospects over long-term gains. In other words, they prioritize profits over people. Many businesses through the pandemic saw an opportunity to grow, so they made the decision to over-hire staff. With a remote workforce that could work from anywhere in the world, companies saw a chance to increase productivity and revenue.

Unfortunately, when the market contracted and the pandemic ended, these companies had far too many workers to be sustainable. Hence, we've seen multiple rounds of layoffs during the past couple years, and this does not seem to be letting up.

Iwata's thinking was strategic and in tune with his teams. He understood the importance of empathy, trust, and safety and knew that prioritizing a healthy culture would not only protect his employees but also lead to better outcomes overall. He also wouldn't have to spend time replacing top talent if he retained them and compensated them well through a tough financial time.

However, his isn't the first story of a CEO making sacrifices to protect their employees.

During World War II, America mobilized and needed rations to feed its soldiers. A brand of spaghetti dinners that we lovingly know as Chef Boyardee was the perfect nonperishable meal to fuel the war effort. Chef Hector Boiardi, the real chef behind the Chef Boyardee brand, was selected by the US government because of his company's experience with the production of canned food.

Boiardi had moved his operations to Milton, Pennsylvania, in 1936, where he began canning his spaghetti and meatballs as well as his beef ravioli. This not only made Chef Boyardee brand products more accessible, but it also employed hundreds of farm workers and revitalized the local economy. Starting in 1942, Boiardi increased his staff to be able to run his facility twenty-four hours a day to meet the demands of the war effort. In 1945, World War II ended, and military rations were no longer needed. Boiardi was left with a critical decision: downsize the company to its prewar size or continue at this scale.

Downsizing would mean he could make more profits, but he would have to lay off thousands of employees who had worked hard to make his company a success during the war. In order to protect his employees' livelihood, he refused to downsize and instead sold his company to a large commercial food company, American Home Products, under the condition that they retain his employees. This decision was difficult, but Boiardi knew that it was the right move. He loved his company and didn't want to sell, but ensuring his employees were taken care of was more important.[2]

The strongest leaders understand that their companies are only successful because of their people. They value and protect their employees at all costs, creating a culture that promotes psychological safety. When faced with a choice between maintaining their own comfort and ensuring the comfort of their teams, they choose to ensure their teams' comfort. In Simon Sinek's viral TED Talk and book *Leaders Eat Last,* he shares a story about a military leader who allowed his unit to eat first, but by the time they were done, there were only crumbs left for him. His unit came back and shared their rations, explaining that they did it because "he would do the same for me."

Managing well doesn't always require self-sacrifice, though. In fact, simple acts of empathy, compassion, and attunement can create connection and enhance company culture.

I remember being invited to give a keynote to a research company on the day of the Supreme Court's *Dobbs* v. *Jackson Women's Health Organization* decision to reverse *Roe v. Wade* (the constitutional right to abortion). The sullen energy in the room was palpable. There were employees on both ends of the political spectrum, and some were struggling with the Court's decision. One by one, people signed into the Zoom call, silently looking down at their desks. I wasn't sure whether I was going to have to address the elephant in the room or if someone within the organization was going to step in.

Being in tune with the dynamics of the team, I sat quietly, waiting for my cue to begin my keynote on burnout, which felt insignificant compared to what everyone was experiencing in that moment. Suddenly, the CEO logged into the meeting and started addressing his staff in an empathetic but somber tone.

"Hey, everyone, thank you all for joining today. I want to take a few minutes to acknowledge that today might be a hard day for many of you. I know that this decision affects millions of people across the country, and I just want to say that I'm so sorry. The reverberations of this decision will be felt for years to come, so if you need to log off or take time off to take care of yourselves, please do so. I'd also like to open up the opportunity for anyone to share, if they'd like to."

I fully expected that it was going to be radio silence. No one's going to speak up about such a touchy topic in a meeting, I thought. But to my surprise, people came off mute and talked about how this would impact them. They talked about their fears for their daughters and their worries about starting families without access to emergency care if something were to go wrong with their pregnancy, and the CEO responded in an attuned manner.

"It makes sense that you're fearful, and I know that this is scary for not only you, but for generations to come. I'm so sorry."

I was shocked. Even though I'd worked with many big-name companies, I'd never seen a team that felt so safe and had a leader who was able to respond in a manner that maintained appropriate boundaries while still providing compassionate care. He didn't know it at the time, but he was modeling what it means to be in tune for his employees.

He also held space for anyone who had opposing views, and he toed the line so as to acknowledge their perspectives, too. It was quite masterful and made me feel even more grateful to collaborate with the company.

Empathy is often pigeonholed as a "soft skill," making it seem nonessential and nice to have, when in reality, it's a power skill that is essential to any high-performing team.

✧

A 2021 study conducted by Catalyst found that 61 percent of employees were likely to report being innovative when they had an empathetic leader, while 76 percent reported feeling engaged at work as a result of their leader's empathy. When they felt valued and respected by their leadership, 62 percent of women of color said they were unlikely to think about leaving their companies. And 50 percent of employees with empathetic leaders reported that their company was inclusive. Lastly, 86 percent of employees said they were able to navigate work and life demands effectively when they had an empathetic leader.[3]

The data doesn't lie. Empathy is good for innovation, engagement, retention, inclusivity, and well-being.

One of the foundational elements of empathy is the ability to listen. It's the skill of putting yourself in someone else's shoes and considering where they are both cognitively and emotionally. It's not listening to respond; it's listening to understand.

Some of the most legendary CEOs gained that title as a result of becoming exceptional listeners. Instead of trying to dictate what to do and where to go next, they connected with the people they were leading to gain perspective. A fantastic example of this is David Abney.

David Abney, who joined UPS in 1974 at age nineteen, became CEO forty years later. He was promoted through the ranks and led more than 480,000 employees. His employees especially respected him because of his ability to listen and hear his teams' feedback. He made it his mission to get in tune with what people really wanted and needed from UPS.

When he first joined UPS as CEO, Abney went on a worldwide listening tour, asking employees and customers what they thought the company should focus on going forward. Taking this step allowed employees and customers to feel both understood and part of the future of UPS, which improved their investment in the brand.

One employee stated, "When David issued a call for ideas, many of which were actually implemented, it was earth-shattering. We couldn't believe leadership was finally listening and taking action on our recommendations."[4]

In a world of leaders who think they know what's best and run the company from an ivory tower, Abney stood out as a leader who was humble enough to receive on-the-ground feedback and then act on it. He wasn't simply considering people's recommendations; he was responding congruently and actively making changes based on the information gathered. Listening is a good first step, but taking action is what's needed to drive change.

I'm not proud to admit it, but when I was invited to consult and deliver keynotes to a finance firm on supporting neurodivergent employees at work, I walked in with my own assumptions about the finance industry. Because the industry isn't known for being the most empathetic or accommodating, I thought this was likely going to be an instance of paying lip service, and nothing would actually change within the company. Many organizations say they want to improve culture or accommodate individuals with disabilities, but then they aren't willing to do the hard, long-term work of changing systems to make it happen.

However, when I met with the HR department to discuss how I could help their organization, I was pleasantly surprised that they genuinely wanted to support their teams. They had sent out a survey asking their employees what they thought would be the most impactful learning initiative, and the response was that their neurodivergent employees were wanting more accommodation.

I presented the keynote, which educated the organization about mental health, neurodivergence, and what accommodations are the most effective, and people were engaged and willing to learn. Still, I was jaded and didn't think anything would actually change. In my mind, this was just another informative talk that would help the individuals, but the systems would remain the same.

To my surprise, the HR department reached out again later to ask me to come back and consult with their team so they could implement what I had taught. When I met with them, they shared that they had already increased their flexibility, they had started having formal accommodations conversations that adapted the specific interventions I had outlined to work for each person, and they were prioritizing psychological safety by informing neurodivergent employees of their rights under privacy laws like HIPAA.

I couldn't believe it. They listened! Not only did they listen to me; they were listening to their employees. They took copious notes during my HR consultation, and they asked thoughtful questions about putting ideas into action. As a result, their employees were able to focus more, they felt like they had more say in their workflow, and their outcomes improved. Not only that, their leaders were thinking unconventionally about how their teams could function best, which drove innovation. It was a win-win.

Innovation is a by-product of managing well because teams are much more likely to be creative and think outside the box when they feel they are supported within their workplace. Filippo Catalano, who was the CIO at Nestlé, shows us how a well-run organization inspires innovation.

Catalano wanted to encourage groundbreaking thinking within his teams, so he created Nestlé's InGenius, a global employee-driven innovation accelerator that has engaged more than sixty-two thousand employees. More than four thousand eight hundred ideas were shared, three hundred prototypes were developed, and sixty-nine projects were taken to market. Catalano's mentality was that empowering his employees to be curious would allow them to come up with new and unique products that could benefit everyone. That proved to be true.

Catalano remarked, "You want to encourage people to be curious, innovative, courageous, and collaborative. This means also empowering our employees and harnessing their passion and knowledge to bring innovation to the company."[5]

His initiative is an example of attuned leadership because he saw an opportunity to connect with what lit up his employees. He didn't try to force them to focus on making his ideas come to life; he instead adapted by providing a platform through which they could develop their own. His teams were crying out for a chance to utilize their knowledge and expertise, and he provided them that chance.

While there are so many examples of companies that are

getting it wrong, there are also a multitude of opportunities to learn from those that are getting it right. It doesn't have to be overcomplicated, and you definitely don't need to be someone's therapist to be working well.

Often, it's the simple interventions that create the greatest impact.

Neurodivergent Tip

Neurodivergent employees are often some of the most dedicated and loyal employees out there. If we're treated well, we'll stick with an organization for many years because flexibility, safety, and security are what many of us desire most.

Brad struggled with social anxiety most of his life, and in-person work interactions were taxing and stressful. He would overthink conversations, isolate himself in his office, and feel the dread build up before team meetings.

He told his boss about his diagnosis, and as an accommodation, Brad was given the opportunity to work remotely. He was thrilled because it meant he wouldn't have to expend a ton of energy on managing his anxiety at work, and he could instead focus that energy on the tasks at hand.

His colleagues observed that having to deal with social pressures was hard for Brad, so when the boss asked to have cameras on during meetings, the team advocated for everyone to have the option to attend meetings with their cameras off. They made the case that everyone would be present and listening intently, but they just wouldn't have to worry about their appearance or making eye contact on the call. The boss took the feedback and permitted people to do whatever made them feel comfortable, which was a huge relief for Brad.

Brad's anxiety levels felt much better managed. He became a top performer in his job, and he felt like his team and his boss really cared about his well-being. They anticipated and attuned to his needs, and Brad became a loyal employee.

While other team members came and went, Brad stayed because he felt safe and comfortable in his work environment. He became one of the company's most valuable IT employees because he was able to quickly problem-solve and walk people through solutions to their technical challenges. It's been five years, and Brad is still going strong.

Brad wasn't ashamed of his diagnosis, but he also made sure he disclosed his disability to a leader he could trust. Instead of waiting until his social anxiety affected his performance, he asked for help early on so adjustments could be made.

The biggest mistake I see the leaders and employees I work with make is that they wait to ask for support until there are performance issues. By that point, performance improvement plans have likely been put into place, and unfortunately, leadership looks at your disclosure as an excuse instead of a legitimate reason for the challenges at hand. It's not right, but it's what happens.

You want to have systems in place soon after you accept a job as a preventative measure versus as a reactionary measure. The accommodations can be adjusted, but prioritize getting them in place once you join.

Attuning to neurodivergent needs means providing accommodations and supports to ensure our success. Having conversations to better understand how we work best is critical because we're not monoliths, and what worked best for Brad may not work best for your neurodivergent team members. Bosses need to find ways to be flexible and adaptable, and colleagues also need to shift how they approach interactions based on the preferences of their neurodivergent teammates.

Asking questions, approaching conversations with curiosity, and responding accordingly is how you create the trust that keeps us committed to your company.

Part III

CHECK-IN

YOU'VE LEARNED HOW to tune in to yourself, you've learned how to manage your emotions, you've learned how to identify and bridge connection gaps, and you've seen some examples of healthy workplaces throughout history. Now it's time to delve into the art of attunement.

The CHECK-IN framework is a step-by-step process for connecting, supporting, and repairing relationships. Of course, you'll need to shift and adapt what you say based on the unique needs of the person you're engaging with, but this framework provides a tried-and-trusted structure for what to say and do when you need guidance on how to show up for others.

Chapter 8

CHECK-IN

Connect

"WE CAN'T WAIT to have you on the team. You're our top candidate." Tessa was elated. She'd been looking to change companies as an accountant, and this was her opportunity to join an organization that seemed to care. The compensation package and benefits were great, and it had a culture of flexible remote work. It checked all the boxes.

Tessa got acclimatized and was rocking at her job. Her bosses had nothing but positive things to say about her as she was meeting deadlines and getting things in order for tax season. All was well.

Unfortunately, a few weeks later, things started to change. Tessa became less communicative. She said she was going to log in to work certain hours, but the software did not show that she was logging in. She didn't have paid time off or sick leave accrued yet, so she just did her best to work when she could. Deadlines were slipping by, and her bosses grew concerned.

"What's going on with Tessa?" they asked the HR manager who had helped hire her. "She's been so flaky lately, and I don't know if she's going to work out for the company."

The HR manager had no idea what was happening but knew she needed to do some outreach. She called Tessa repeatedly, but Tessa didn't pick up or respond to the calls. Days passed, and she grew concerned that Tessa had abandoned the job.

Leadership said, "Wow, what a mistake to hire Tessa. She seemed good, but she clearly doesn't care about this job or working. How disrespectful to not even respond to our outreach. That's not the kind of person we want working here." They prepared to let Tessa go, but the HR manager insisted on calling one more time.

This time, Tessa did respond. The HR manager felt pressure to come down hard on Tessa, as other leaders felt she was being too easy on her.

"Tessa, where have you been? We've been trying to contact you for days, and we can't continue to have someone with your level of disregard or lack of dedication on this team. We have goals that we have to meet, and your lack of communication and follow-through are completely unacceptable. Do you have anything to say for yourself?"

Tessa apologized profusely. "I'm sorry that I haven't been responsive. A few days ago, I had a sharp pain in my left abdomen that became excruciating. I tried to take over-the-counter painkillers, but nothing helped. I was sent to the ER, and they ran a bunch of tests to see what was going on. They recommended that I get a CT scan and an MRI, and it turns out that they found something. I had a mass in my colon the size of a lemon that was causing the abdominal pain. They did emergency surgery and removed the mass, but when they did the biopsy, they found that it's stage III colon cancer. I've been in the hospital ever since, which is why I wasn't able to respond. I'm undergoing chemotherapy and radiation every day here, and I just couldn't get on the phone to explain things."

The HR manager was stunned. She sat in silence for a few seconds and had no idea what to say. She had come in ready to fire Tessa under the assumption that she had abandoned the job, but now she knew the real reason for Tessa's absence.

"I . . . uh . . . I'm so sorry to hear this, Tessa. I had no idea you were going through all of this, and your lack of communication makes so much more sense now. Let's figure out what kinds of support you'll need at work so you can focus on your treatment."

The HR manager felt horrible. She'd laid into Tessa without any context or understanding of what was going on. She and the team made decisions based on a number of assumptions that led to the conclusion that Tessa was a bad employee who needed to be let go. Yes, Tessa could have been more communicative, but had her leaders taken the time to be curious and recognize this behavior was out of character for the person they hired, they could have saved themselves the embarrassment of making such a major misstep.

A few months later, when Tessa was well again, she put in her resignation. She never forgot how she was characterized and treated during such a dark time. The trust was destroyed, and there was no rebuilding that.

Too often, we allow judgment and assumptions to be the

North Stars for our actions. We jump to conclusions based on incomplete and insufficient evidence to back up what we think is happening. We fill in the gaps incorrectly and then pay the price down the line.

What if instead we could pause to be curious instead of judgmental? What if we could be information seekers instead of information shirkers?

Asking good questions is essential for any successful relationship, and this holds especially true for our work relationships. The goal isn't to just treat symptoms, it's to address the root problem, and questions allow you to connect with the deeper problems at hand.

People are willing to open up and share as long as we approach questions with openness and empathy. As Brené Brown's research underscores, connection requires vulnerability, and vulnerability is a risk.[1] If employees receive an empathetic response, then they determine that the risk was worthwhile and they'll share again. But if they receive a judgmental response, then they will never take the risk of opening up again. They'll quiet quit, and one day, seemingly out of the blue, they'll give you their resignation.

You can tell that you're approaching a conversation with an open-minded curiosity when you ask open-ended questions. Close-ended questions truncate conversations and require only a yes or no response. They show that you're looking for confirmation of what you already believe to be true, and that you're not interested in better understanding what's really happening under the surface.

Close-ended questions sound like "Did you know that you have to give us a week's notice to take time off?" or "Can you handle taking on another project?" or "Have you decided on whether you want to work alongside the other team?"

They're terrible questions because they don't tell you anything. These types of questions don't open up the pathway for connection because the person being asked can just say yes or no and provide no additional context for why they're responding in a certain way or what might have informed their decision.

One time, I missed the deadline for submitting a statement of interest for a position that I really wanted. I had been punctual, a strong contributor, and a great candidate for the role, so when the deadline came and went, I felt awful. It was out of character for me, as I'm someone who plans ahead and will work tirelessly to ensure that I get tasks done by the expected timeline. Nothing is worse to me than letting people down or not being true to my word.

I ended up pulling an all-nighter to get the job done, and it was submitted a couple hours after the closing deadline. I breathed a sigh of relief, but I knew I was probably going to hear about this from the boss.

Lo and behold, my boss scheduled a meeting with me shortly after I submitted my application. My gut told me I was in trouble and that I might have screwed up my chances of being selected.

She logged into the meeting, and I could tell from her demeanor that she was already on the defense. With no check-in or warmth, she started in. "So, I see that you submitted your application. Did you realize that you were late in submitting it?"

"Yes, I realize that," I replied.

"Did you know that everyone else got theirs in the day before, well ahead of the deadline?"

"I do," I replied.

"So do you think that the deadline doesn't apply to you?" she asked.

"That's not the case. I think the deadline does apply to me; I just had a personal crisis and couldn't get it finished in time," I explained.

"Well, clearly you don't think so, because otherwise you would have submitted it on time. I expected better from you, and I'm disappointed." It felt like a parent was scolding me. She busted out the *d* word: *disappointed.* Not once did she ask me why I was late in submitting or what was the personal crisis.

Fighting back tears, I shared, "Well, my father-in-law suddenly passed away, and I didn't get a chance to get it done. It's been really hard, and I am normally on top of things, but his death and supporting my husband as he grieved losing his father threw everything off. I thought you would have given me a little bit of grace considering that I've never missed anything before in my years of working with you."

She became even more defensive. She had made so many assumptions and had gotten herself so worked up without ever considering what was going on in my world. She said, "I'm sorry for your loss, but you could have communicated with me and let me know. I expected that from you, and it's not a good look. It shows your lack of commitment to the work that we're doing here, and that's not what I want in a leader."

What part of "suddenly passed away" didn't she understand? Why so many low blows? It felt like all she cared about was being right and reprimanding me for not doing things perfectly. Granted, this wasn't my best moment as an employee, but I was also dealing with the loss of a parent figure and wasn't operating as my best self. The attunement, compassion, and empathy went out of the window. I knew there was no point in continuing the conversation.

"I'll be sure to keep you in the loop next time." Luckily, there was no next time because I decided to leave shortly after that conversation.

This discussion could have gone very differently had she asked open-ended, curious questions. She could have said, "I noticed that you missed the submission deadline for the role. What happened that caused the delay?" Or she could have said, "It's unlike you to miss a deadline like you did the other day. Could you tell me more about what's going on?"

Simple, open-ended questions coupled with an attuned, empathetic response could have transformed the way the conversation ended up going. I was ready to dedicate years to that organization, but once I saw the leader's response to this situation and others, I knew I couldn't ignore the glaring red flags.

I didn't trust that she would be supportive and understanding if, God forbid, I were to suddenly get sick or have something happen that would require me to focus on life outside her business.

Other examples of open-ended questions include questions that start with *what, how,* or *why.*

"How did you feel when . . . ?"

"What are your thoughts on . . . ?"

"Why did you choose . . . ?"

"What did you think about . . . ?"

When the person responds with an answer, don't just let the conversation die there. Ask follow-up questions to continue the dialogue and further your understanding of their experience.

These include "Tell me more about . . . ," "Say more about . . . ," "Help me better understand . . . ," "Could you dive deeper into . . . ," and "I'm curious about . . ."

I know this sounds simple, but in practice, it takes work. I can tell you that so many teams struggle with going beneath the surface to truly understand one another. It's much more comfortable to ask close-ended questions or to respond with yes or no, but sticking to what's comfortable stifles connection.

The quality of outreach matters much more than the quantity of outreach, so make it count.

Neurodivergent Tip

Sometimes, it can take a minute for us neurodivergent people to process what is happening and what is being asked. We're trying to take in everything that is going on in the interaction and simultaneously trying to identify what we think, feel, and need to do in that moment.

Michelle, who struggles with anxiety, and her team coleader, Stacy, were discussing the team's feedback regarding an initiative they put forward to help to better organize their teams. Michelle noticed that the team was disjointed because there weren't enough touchpoints throughout the week, and people were often feeling lost and overwhelmed while navigating their work assignments on their own.

After speaking with a couple colleagues, Michelle decided to schedule Zoom meetings once a day for thirty minutes so everyone could share what they were working on, and the team could provide thoughts or suggestions about difficult problems that arose. In her mind, this would strengthen team cohesion and lead to fewer miscommunications along the way.

Michelle experimented with this approach for a few weeks, and it seemed like it was going well. But in reality, the team went behind Michelle's back to Stacy and complained. They felt like daily meetings were too much and that they were wasting time sitting and talking about their work instead of doing it.

Stacy brought up these concerns to Michelle in their manager's meeting, and Michelle was stunned. No one had communicated anything to her, and she thought that these meetings were actually helping.

In an effort to better understand Michelle's viewpoint, Stacy started firing off a series of questions.

"So, help me understand the rationale behind these meetings. What do you think about the team's feedback? Why did you choose a daily frequency instead of a weekly frequency for the meetings?"

Michelle found herself frozen. Her anxiety started to escalate, and she could feel herself beginning to panic inside. She was still processing that the team didn't like the meetings and that they had expressed these concerns to Stacy instead of to her, and now she felt like she was under Stacy's microscope. She couldn't answer the questions fast enough, and now she was feeling incompetent as a leader.

When you're approaching conversations with curiosity with anyone, but especially with people who are neurodivergent, be sure you're not overwhelming them with questions. Your intentions may be good, in that you're trying to better understand their thought process and their perspective, but often, people need more time to process and take in what is being said so they can answer accurately and adequately.

Instead, ask a question and then pause for the response before moving on to the next. If the person seems like they're struggling to provide an answer, validate that they may need more time by saying something like "I know I shared a lot with you and you might need a moment to process, so take your time."

For some people, they may need to have a follow-up meeting with you after they've gathered their thoughts to share what they are truly thinking and feeling. They need to not only make sense of the emotional experience, but they also need to rationally think through their approach, so a follow-up meeting can be a more effective strategy.

If you're the person who is neurodivergent and feels overwhelmed by the barrage of questions, it's okay to ask for what you need, which in this case is to take each question one at a time. You might say something like "I want to make sure I thoroughly answer all of your questions. Could you repeat them one by one so I can address each fully?" This approach simultaneously advocates for what you need and shows the person on the other end that you want to be intentional in your responses.

I'd also encourage you to regulate your nervous system using some of the tools discussed in earlier chapters. It's difficult to think clearly when your mind and body feel stressed and overwhelmed, so remember, calm body = calm mind. Some examples of tools you could use include breathing, grounding yourself by noticing your feet planted firmly on the ground, and clasping your hands so you don't fidget.

Chapter 9

CHECK-IN

Hold Space

WE SAT DOWN at a table within the organic grocery store with our hot line food in hand. I wasn't sure where our conversation was going to lead, but I knew I needed to be honest with her.

I was meeting with my boss on a Saturday afternoon after preparing all morning to share about my decision to leave my job. I had rehearsed and rehearsed again so I could give my rationale while still being respectful and appreciative. But the red flags were waving right in front of my face, and I knew I had to go.

My first week on the job, I was elated to meet the team during our team meeting. Everyone seemed so nice, so I couldn't wait to call this place my work home for at least the next couple years. After enduring a workplace that went from healthy to unhealthy during the course of three years, I craved stability and a different work dynamic.

But as that initial meeting proceeded, I could immediately see that I was hired to help get the team out of the depths of despair. The team sarcastically joked, "Nidhi is here now and can save us!" I immediately tensed up because I knew that underneath the sarcasm was truth. I had barely set up my office, and now I was expected to pick up the pieces from the others who had left.

They spent the whole meeting talking about how their jobs were unsustainable and that they were all burned out. They described how unhappy they were, and many of them threatened to leave if they didn't get relief soon. I saw the writing on the wall, and I was not about to become the martyr of the organization. But I was stuck. I had moved more than a hundred miles to join this company, so I needed to stick it out for a while.

I stayed for a little over a year before I started burning out myself. The caseloads were through the roof, everyone was spread too thin, and my best friend had recently passed away and I was still grieving that loss. I didn't want to job hop, but past experiences had taught me that no job was worth sacrificing my mental health.

The one silver lining of this company was that my boss, Karen, and the team were empathetic and supportive. They always had my back, and they made it a point to check in and listen to what was going on in my world.

Normally, I'd just hand over a written resignation and call it a day, but my boss's grace and understanding toward me during the course of that year made me feel like a conversation was needed.

Before we sat down, she gave me the warmest hug.

"Hey, Nidhi, it's so good to see you! I've been looking forward to meeting up. I know we don't usually get a chance to connect outside of work."

I started to doubt my decision to let her know I was leaving. She was so nice, and I felt terrible about moving on to another role because I knew it would put her in a tough position again. There was so much work to get done, and I wouldn't be there to carry some of the weight.

I mustered the courage and said, "I really appreciate you meeting me. I wanted to talk to you about work, and some of the stressors. It's been a lot to balance with everything going on in my personal life."

She replied, "Oh yeah, things have been so intense at work, and I know you're also going through losing your best friend. I lost my dad a year ago, and my mom is getting older, too, so I totally understand how hard it is to manage everything when you also have emotional stress outside of work."

What the hell was this?! I had to pinch myself because I'd so seldom experienced this type of support in the workplace. Normally, my bosses were lacking empathy and compassion, but Karen anticipated how hard things had been for me, and she validated what I was feeling without my even having to put it into words.

I could feel my anxiety starting to melt away. "That's exactly it. I'm doing my best to balance it all, but it's been really overwhelming. I feel like I'm falling behind. I normally could handle all this, but with the grief added on, I think it's just really hard. I'm thinking the best thing for my mental and physical health is to go into private practice, where I can have more say about when and how I work."

I braced myself for the backlash. She was understanding a moment ago, but in my experience, things start to shift when you let the boss know that they're going to be down a team member. The team was already drowning, and I was about to take away one of the remaining life rafts by leaving. I've seen leaders smile and act supportive but then turn on me down the line.

She paused to take in what I had shared. The silence felt like it lasted forever even though it was only for a few seconds.

She leaned in and softly replied, "Oh, Nidhi, I'm so sorry you're going through all of this. I fully support you. Your health and well-being have to come first, and this job is pretty unreasonable. I've burned out, most of the team has burned out, and I'd hate for that to happen to you, too. You've done a great job taking on so much for the team, but you've got to protect yourself, and if it was me in your position, I'd be leaving, too."

Before I could reply, Karen embraced me with another hug and reminded me that it was okay. She wasn't mad; she wasn't disappointed; she just understood.

I didn't see it in that moment, but in retrospect, Karen was repairing the damage done all the times before when bosses didn't hold space for me. She knew how to shift her body language, tone of voice, and words to connect with me.

Even though this was a hard conversation, Karen didn't lean away like so many others had done. When we experience discomfort, we quite literally try to put distance between ourselves and the discomfort, which shows up in our body language. We cross our arms and legs, we shift away, we fidget, and we wriggle in our seats. Karen didn't do any of those things. She maintained a calm, connected demeanor; her facial expressions showed concern and compassion; and she made me feel safe. My anxiety lessened because her physical response was grounded and centered, which then made me feel grounded and centered. Remember, our minds and bodies sync up to each other, and her ability to stay present and attentive made a massive impact on dissipating my nervousness.

Karen softened her tone, literally reduced the volume of her voice, and spoke in a slower, more regulated cadence. She could have responded in an amped-up, stressed way, pointing out all the reasons that running your own business can be overwhelming, but instead, she chose to be the calm in the storm. Behaving in this way also helped me feel like she was able to connect with me and that her focus was on my well-being versus what would happen next at work. She didn't do this in a way that felt fake or exaggerated; she just naturally understood that this type of conversation warranted an empathetic response.

These kinds of behavioral shifts lead to co-regulation, or the process of regulating emotions and behaviors with the help of a supportive person. In essence, each helps the other manage their feelings. By creating a space for me express what I had been keeping inside for so long, Karen assisted me in regulating my thoughts, feelings, and behaviors. My anxiety de-escalated, and I was able to talk through my rationale for coming to this conclusion.

Even though I was delivering information that was not what she wanted to hear, how Karen responded to my resignation was exactly the type of validation I had needed throughout my career. She didn't make me feel guilty or talk about how hard it would be to replace me. She focused on what I needed.

She knew that this was not an easy decision for me, and she validated that I needed to prioritize my mental and physical health. I had uprooted my life to come to work for this agency, but life had other plans for me. Her support and understanding showed me that she genuinely cared, and her affirmation that she'd be making the same choice if she was in my shoes confirmed that I was doing the right thing. She encouraged me and offered support as I navigated the new terrain of starting my own business, as she had previously owned her own practice. This created a closer connection.

These may sound like simple steps, but simple actions can make a massive impact when holding space. We lose self-awareness in moments of stress, and we don't respond as our best selves. Many leaders forget to acknowledge the humanity of the people on their teams, and it creates chasms instead of connection. They expect work and life to be separated, but the reality is that they are inextricably linked. We have to strengthen our interpersonal skills instead of expecting people to only focus on work while at work. Asking people to compartmentalize is a cop-out because it's a reflection of our inability to hold space.

Basic skills are critical skills, and we have to do the work to hone them.

Neurodivergent Tip

For many neurodivergent folks, our intuition is spot-on. We can spot genuine empathy versus the fake niceties of disingenuous compassion. We can also sense when someone is trying to use empathy as a way to patronize and feel bad for us versus feeling what we're experiencing alongside us.

After years of thinking about homeownership, Preston bought a house because his boss told him that he would be getting a promotion in the next thirty days. Preston had received the tentative offer letter outlining his salary increase and improved job title. All that was left was for HR to formally complete the process.

Preston was thrilled by the good news, and he saw an opportunity to accomplish a lifelong dream by buying a new house. After all, a significant pay bump was coming, and he could finally afford to take on a mortgage instead of paying rent to his landlord.

During the next thirty days, he completed the closing process and had the keys in his hand to move in. He arranged for a moving company to pick up his furniture, and by his estimates, he would have his family settled into their new home within a couple of weeks.

He returned to work excited to share the news. In his one-on-one with his boss, he talked about how grateful he was for the opportunity to grow within the company, and that this promotion was life-changing for him. His boss stopped in his tracks and looked pale as a ghost. Preston could sense that something was wrong.

"Is everything okay?" he asked. His boss shakily replied, "Well, we pushed the promotion through to HR and everything was looking good. But then I received an email from HR this morning stating that there were budget cuts, and we'll have to delay the promotion until the next quarter. I'm so sorry, Preston. I had no idea this would happen."

Preston was stunned. He couldn't believe what he was hearing. The house was already bought because he had been assured that this position was a guaranteed deal. Now, he could see his dreams crumbling before his eyes.

After the meeting, Preston stopped by his colleague Jodi's office to vent about what had just happened. He needed to take a few minutes to process the news he'd just gotten, and he figured since he and Jodi had worked together for years, she'd be a good person to go to.

Preston shared this earth-shattering news with Jodi, and she immediately jumped in with what she thought was empathy.

"Holy crap, Preston, I'd hate to be you right now. I feel really bad for what you're going through."

Preston thanked Jodi for her response, but as he returned to his office, something felt off inside. It felt like Jodi was just acknowledging his misfortune instead of sharing in his emotions. It almost came across like she felt sorry for him, and that felt condescending to Preston.

When you're holding space for people who are neurodivergent, be sure to approach the conversation from a place of empathy versus sympathy. We don't want you to feel sorry for us; we want you to understand what we're going through.

Sympathy involves feeling sorry about the other person's situation and emotions, but focusing on one's own emotions instead of the other person's. Sympathy sounds like "I feel sorry for you," which focuses on your feelings about their experience.

Empathy involves listening and validating the other person's emotions, trying to understand their perspective, and listening without judgment. Empathy sounds like "This sucks. Your disappointment and shock are totally warranted," which focuses on normalizing their emotional experience.

When we sense empathy, we open up and share more. When we sense sympathy, we close down and withdraw. Be sure you're making your interactions about understanding the other person's emotions instead of inserting your own into the situation.

If you're the neurodivergent person who is consistently on the receiving end of sympathy instead of empathy from a colleague, it might be a sign that they're not the best person to go to with your concerns. You should make an attempt to communicate what you specifically need, which is for them to listen and validate your feelings versus feeling sorry for you, but if they continue to go to a place of sympathy instead of empathy, it's okay to decide that they're not the best source of support.

That doesn't mean that you need to cut them out completely. It simply means that they may not have the capacity and skills to provide the type of support that you desire, and others may be better equipped to give you that support. Kind, good-hearted people can have difficulties with holding space for challenging situations, and their inability to provide support is not necessarily a reflection on you or on their desire to be there for you.

It's a reflection of where they are on their own emotional journey.

Chapter 10

CHECK-IN

Explore with Empathy

As Karen and I continued our dialogue, she got really curious about my next steps in opening up a business. I didn't feel like she was prying into my plans to get more information out of me, but rather she genuinely wanted to meet me where I was.

"I'm excited that you're opening up your own practice. What inspired you to become a business owner?" she asked.

After taking a moment to piece together a thoughtful response, I replied, "It's been a lifelong dream of mine to venture out on my own. I'd like to take the years of experience I've accrued from working with the government to give back to the community. Plus, there's flexibility when it's your own business. I know there are set hours for our agency and set expectations when it comes to output. Some days, when the grief knocks me down, it's hard to get up early to work. If I owned my own business, I'd have autonomy and choice over when I work, with whom I work, and how much I work. That feels right in this moment."

"That makes sense. You have more control to adapt your workload to match the ebbs and flows that come with grief, and that flexibility is something you really only get when you're calling the shots in your business. What types of supports would be helpful as you transition out?"

I hadn't thought this part through yet. I had just come to terms with leaving, but I had no idea about transition plans or what needed to happen in the four weeks leading up to my departure.

I hesitated. "Uhh, I'm not exactly sure. I haven't gotten that far, so I'll have to give that some thought."

This type of frozen reaction often happens when tough news is delivered or critical feedback is given. Your team members may not immediately have a response and may not say much because they are slowly processing what you've shared. Instead of barraging them with questions about whether they agree with your feedback or asking them how they might take action, pause and allow them the space to think about what you've shared. Giving them this menu of options takes the pressure off and lowers the stakes in the conversation.

"That's totally fine, take your time. Just some food for thought—I could support by shifting some of your clients off your plate. I'm happy to cover some of your meetings so you can focus on getting documentation done before you leave. I could also let the team know on your behalf so you don't have to stress thinking about how you want to let folks know. If there's something else that you think of, let's talk and I'll see how I can support."

I could feel myself breathing a sigh of relief. Karen presenting me with this menu of options helped me move through the frozen feeling of not knowing what to ask for. I didn't want to seem like I was unprepared, but I was still feeling a little overwhelmed with the conversation, so I wasn't able to think things through like I normally would. Having some potential options laid out helped.

This is a common strategy when exploring with empathy and curiosity. Every step of the way, Karen took a moment to ask instead of assuming. She gave me a variety of options, which empowered me to have agency and choice in deciding next steps. She didn't pressure me to make a decision right then and there. She gave me the opportunity to take time to process, and she offered additional support if I thought of something else that I needed.

She understood where I was coming from, and she validated my reasons. She curiously asked, "I know this will be your first time in private practice. Would it be helpful to talk through the process? Or I can just listen while you talk about how you're approaching things. I used to have my own practice, but I don't want to assume that you want advice."

As a future business owner, I greatly appreciated her willingness to support and share her knowledge. Even though I was leaving her organization, she was invested in my success. Most importantly, she didn't assume I wanted help. She asked for permission to share, which put me in the driver's seat of the interaction.

Exploring empathetically is about taking a learner/listener

stance. You don't need to have all the answers or all the solutions, but you do need to take the time to ask instead of assuming, offer options, and determine which supports are most needed by the other person.

You may think you know what someone else wants, but ultimately, only they know what they need.

Neurodivergent Tip

Agency and autonomy can often be even more important for neurodivergent people. It's critical that we have a say in how people help and that we feel in control of what supports are put into place.

Elaine had a sensory processing disorder and struggled with the chaos of in-person work. She had a difficult time focusing and feeling grounded when there were team conversations, meetings, and the clacking of keyboards all around her.

When she shared her diagnosis with her colleagues, they expressed empathy and compassion, and they wanted to do what they could do to reduce the overwhelm for her. Collectively, they got together and decided that they would leave Elaine alone and limit their interactions with her so she could feel more comfortable. Unfortunately, no one communicated this to Elaine.

Each day, Elaine came to her cubicle and sat down and no one interacted with her. People stopped saying hi, they stopped asking her for help, and they just left her by herself in her cubicle at all times.

Elaine started to feel isolated and like she was not part of the team. The shift seemed to happen after she shared her diagnosis, so she started to regret ever talking about her struggles with the team. She enjoyed the interpersonal interactions with her colleagues; it was just the ambient noise that was throwing her off. But her team had decided that they would help her in their own way.

Eventually, Elaine asked one of her close friends on the team why everyone had stopped talking to her. Her friend explained that they were trying to support her by giving her space to focus and they had come to the conclusion that the best way to do that was to leave her alone.

Elaine was taken aback. She had never asked to be supported in this way, and her colleagues just assumed that what she needed was isolation, when in reality, occasional social interaction helped her feel like a part of a community. She explained to her friend that people saying hi or asking for help was never the problem, and that these interactions were meaningful and important to her. It was the fact that she had a cubicle with no door, so when she needed to focus, there was no way to dampen the noise.

The team got the feedback from Elaine's friend, and they felt silly for pulling away from Elaine so suddenly. They went back to engaging with her regularly, and Elaine felt like she belonged once again.

Too often, the supports that are identified as accommodations for neurodivergent people are not actually what they desire or need. They're cookie-cutter solutions that are determined based on other people's understanding of the condition.

Neurodivergent folks need to have a say about how other people show up and support them. We're especially sensitive to not being included in the decision-making process, because for many of us, when we were growing up, decisions were made without our input. Sometimes, we were infantilized, and providers, family members, and friends assumed that we did not know what was best for ourselves, so they did what they thought was best.

Be sure to have conversations and be especially open to learning how you show up and support your neurodivergent colleagues. Autonomy and self-determination are critical, and we need to be able to provide feedback about what works and what doesn't.

As neurodivergent employees and leaders, we also have to advocate for our own needs. Workplaces are required to provide us reasonable accommodations in order for us to thrive in our roles, but they can't read our minds or know what's most helpful unless we communicate it. If colleagues and leaders are offering you options that do not feel supportive, it's okay to suggest alternatives.

If you benefit from having quiet time to work after meetings, that's a reasonable request. If you have therapy sessions or medical appointments during business hours, it's okay to ask for time off to attend those appointments. If having a space to work in person is beneficial, you can see if a fully remote role will allow you to come into the office once or twice a week.

The worst that HR and your boss can say to your requests is no, but there's also the possibility they could say yes. Unfortunately, if you don't ask, the guaranteed answer is no.

Chapter 11

CHECK-IN

Congruently Respond

NISHA WORKED FOR her company for three years, and on every performance review, she received an "exceeds expectations" rating. She was well liked on the team, she was always the first to help out when team members were swamped, and she showed strong leadership skills. When she was hired, her boss, Sammie, saw tons of potential for Nisha to move into management positions right away, and Nisha was poised to get the rewards that she had been seeking throughout her career. Nisha made it clear in her interview that upward mobility in the organization was critical to her, and that she wanted to take on a leadership role within the first few years of joining. After all, she had more than ten years of experience under her belt. The leadership team assured her that there were opportunities for her to move up.

During the first couple of years, Nisha made it a point to share her accomplishments with Sammie and to learn and grow into her role. Nisha asked her boss about what specific markers would help her know that she was on track to meet her goals for advancement. Sammie laid out the path forward, including specific performance metrics, communication expectations, and skill sets that Nisha would need to master.

Nisha had her eyes on the prize and asked Sammie to mentor and guide her in improving her skills so she could increase her chances of moving up within the next year. Sammie enthusiastically agreed to help her and told her that they could meet every other week to specifically focus on leadership development and management skills. Nisha was thrilled. The promotion she had always wanted but never got at her last job finally felt within her grasp.

After this conversation, Nisha followed up via email to start scheduling the recurring meetings with her boss. Sammie sent her calendar invites to hold the space for the meeting, and Nisha started to prepare questions and get ready for this mentorship relationship. Nisha wanted to know all about the systems within the organization, the ways to navigate team dynamics, and how to lead teams. She had never gotten experience leading others and wanted to learn from her boss, who had done it for many years.

When the first meeting came around, Sammie showed up twenty minutes late and was frazzled. Nisha asked questions, but Sammie seemed distracted and mentally unavailable. They only had twenty-five minutes to talk, and Nisha felt rushed. Given that projects and the current workload were more demanding for everyone, Nisha chalked it up to Sammie just having an off day.

One week later, Nisha followed up to be sure Sammie was good to meet for their scheduled mentorship session. Sammie said she'd be available to meet, but then thirty minutes before the meeting time, Sammie suddenly canceled due to a conflicting meeting. Nisha tried to reschedule, and Sammie told her she'd let her know by the end of the week when she'd be available.

Nisha checked her email daily, but Sammie never followed up. She didn't want to bother Sammie or annoy her, so she held off on sending the email until the following week to see if they could reschedule and find a consistent time to meet. After a couple days, Sammie eventually responded, but she was noncommittal, saying she was very busy and having a hard time finding space to fit Nisha in. Sammie paused the meetings indefinitely.

Nisha felt betrayed. Not only had she made it abundantly clear in her interview two years before that she needed to move up in the ranks, but she was also doing everything she was told to do in order to get the promotion. Sammie's lack of follow-through on her promise to mentor was eroding the trust between them.

Sammie was failing to deliver, and her actions were incongruent with her words.

We are constantly gauging who is trustworthy and who is untrustworthy. Every interaction adds or detracts from that fragile foundation of trust. When stated values and actions don't match up, that incongruence cuts deep.

In a study published in the *International Journal of Wellbeing*, incongruence between personal and work values, like when people's attitudes, preferences, and behaviors don't match up with the priorities they wish to be recognized for in the workplace, can impact an employee's ability to find meaning in their job. This incongruence also impacts supervisor-employee relationships, reduces opportunities for career advancement, and influences whether employees show up authentically. The lack of authenticity affects their job satisfaction as well.[1]

In Nisha's example, because she valued being recognized for her hard work and efforts in both her personal and professional life, but her job did not recognize and follow through on her wish to be given recognition in the form of a promotion, this incongruence led to lower job satisfaction and impacted her relationship with her supervisor.

Another example of this mismatch is if someone values lower levels of stimulation in their personal lives and likes a slower pace, but their job requires high levels of stimulation and a faster pace—the gap between what's desired and the reality of the work will also affect job satisfaction.

It's in everyone's best interests to behave in alignment with defined values. If you state in job interviews and during the course of an employee's time within your organization that your company prioritizes career advancement and professional development, then you have to follow through by providing promotion and training opportunities to prove that your company operates in alignment with that stated value.

Reduced budgets and time constraints are usually part of the rationale for delaying advancement when an employee has met all the requirements, but that lack of follow-through is detrimental in the long term and diminishes trust within the team. Instead, find ways to be transparent about any roadblocks, and create an alternate plan that still allows the employee to move up. If you cannot provide a pay increase and title change right away, then develop a plan to incrementally improve the salary and advocate for the title change to reflect the increased work they are taking on. Asking people to do more work for free is not the move you want to make.

Congruence does not just relate to career advancement. Your ability to follow through on smaller, day-to-day promises matters, too. If you commit to covering a meeting for your colleague or taking a task off their plate, then you have to follow through on that promise. If you say you'll speak up to defend a coworker who's being targeted in the group meeting, then you have to speak up, even if it's difficult.

Your team members' faith in you is tenuous, and becoming a person who is viewed as inconsistent is hard to shake off. It can be death by a thousand cuts.

Each instance of incongruence erodes trust, and trust is much easier to maintain than to regain.

Neurodivergent Tip

With so many neurodivergent people taking what you say at face value and trusting that you mean what you say, you have to be especially mindful of congruently responding when you agree to do something for a neurodivergent colleague.

Quentin, who is autistic, needed someone to take on creating a proposal for a client because he was swamped with working on delivering projects to his current clients. He asked the team in their weekly touch-base whether someone could help, and Rudy told Quentin that he could probably step in and take care of it. As a more concrete thinker, Quentin saw this as a done deal. He thanked Rudy profusely and crossed off the client proposal from his mental checklist.

Two weeks later, on the proposal's due date, Quentin checked in with Rudy to be sure he had submitted it to the client. Rudy looked surprised. He hadn't submitted to the client because he didn't think that he had formally agreed to take on the work.

Quentin started getting stressed, and he reminded Rudy that he had agreed to step in and take care of it two weeks ago. Rudy was confused because he never said he would definitely take it off Quentin's plate. Rudy said he could probably do it, and he assumed that Quentin knew that meant he was not committing fully.

At the eleventh hour, Quentin scrambled to get the proposal completed, and he vowed to never trust Rudy again. He felt let down, and it came across that Rudy was quibbling over semantics as a way to excuse the fact that he hadn't completed the work. This incongruence between what was said and what was done led to Quentin losing trust in Rudy, and he didn't ask for help from him again.

Clear communication is critical to relationships with neurodivergent colleagues. Had Rudy said, "I can probably take it on, but I'll need to check my calendar to ensure I have space," Quentin wouldn't have banked on Rudy helping out.

Direct, open communication is needed in order for there to be a level setting for all parties, and saying that you'll probably do something leaves a gray area that is difficult for more concrete thinkers. It's especially damaging to relationships with neurodivergent folks because we've experienced this incongruence frequently in our lives. Many of us have had people make promises and not uphold them and then we're told that we misunderstood.

For concrete thinkers, it's important for communications to be black and white so people know what to expect.

If you're the neurodivergent person who may struggle with reading between the lines and understanding the nuance of these interactions, it's okay to ask for clarification. It might feel like you're asking too many questions or digging into the details too much, but that type of information is important for managing your expectations.

In a situation like Quentin's with Rudy, you could tell him in the meeting that you'd like to schedule a quick chat to touch base with him and hammer out the details, or have an email conversation that sets up a game plan. That way, you have the specific timeline in your inbox and you can reference it if you have additional questions. It also helps the other person better understand what they are taking on, so they can have a more realistic estimation of whether they can meet the deadlines, and if they're unable to do it, they can tell you then and there.

When you start to feel weird about the follow-up communications, remember that if someone isn't clear, then it's their responsibility to clarify.

Chapter 12

CHECK-IN

Know How to Repair

THE BOMBSHELL EXPOSÉ shocked everyone who read it.

In 2017, former Uber engineer Susan Fowler published a blog post that highlighted Uber's toxic work culture. She shared experiences of sexual harassment, discrimination, and a lack of accountability from HR leaders within the organization.

Employees were pitted against one another in order to achieve results, and they were encouraged to undermine each other, which created a culture of fear and retaliation against anyone who was a whistleblower. The cutthroat environment and inability of employees to speak out about mistreatment led to several lawsuits and multiple investigations into workplace misconduct.[1]

Everyone was astounded by the mistreatment Uber workers

faced and the lack of intervention from leadership. It seemed that so many people in positions of power had turned a blind eye, and now it was coming to a head.

The scandal led to an internal investigation. Executives were released from their roles, and the CEO at the time, Travis Kalanick, resigned. The entire organization faced a cataclysmic shake-up.

We're in 2026 now, and Uber has repaired its brand reputation and become the biggest rideshare platform in the world. So how did it do it?

Uber didn't know it, but it followed a repair framework called AVP: acknowledge, validate, plan.

First, Uber took accountability and acknowledged the toxic culture that existed within the organization. It validated the employees' concerns and did not continue to bury the grim realities of working for the company. For many of the people who were impacted, Uber provided settlements, which validated that their experiences were real and deserving of repair.

Then, it created a plan for changing the systemic issues that led to people feeling unsafe speaking up, including getting rid of the person at the helm of the toxicity. Dara Khosrowshahi, who was known to prioritize ethical leadership and culture change, was hired as CEO. This led to firing more than twenty employees who were involved in workplace misconduct, which was key in showing that the culture was going to shift.[2]

Then the company examined and audited its workplace culture, which led to implementing stronger HR policies, including mandatory leadership training and improving reporting procedures to ensure people had the appropriate channels to speak up without fear of retribution.

Finally, it needed to repair trust with the public. Uber launched a campaign called "Moving Forward" in which it strived to improve consumer trust and transparency. The company also needed to repair trust within its teams, and it took the time to do that.

Repair is needed at all levels of a company. Whether it's a major scandal like the one Uber faced or the smaller transgressions we see every day in the workplace, repair is what helps organizations recover from their mistakes.

In fact, in many ways, the trust within a team can significantly impact interpersonal dynamics and team cohesion, and once trust is lost, it needs to be repaired.

Derek and Hector's story is a great example of this.

"I know everyone is stressed right now, especially with the upcoming acquisition and restructuring of the company. You all have been sharing your concerns with me, and I know Hector mentioned last week that he is especially concerned about upper management targeting him for not meeting some of the sales metrics. Many of you have expressed similar concerns, so I want you all to know that I've got your back. I'll be defending my team and doing my best to make sure everyone gets to stay, even if leadership makes cuts."

The team supervisor, Derek, passionately delivered this feedback during the weekly huddle, and his team appreciated his directness, given the undercurrent of fear everyone felt. The writing was on the wall; some roles were going to become redundant, and it was inevitable that not everyone would have a job by the time the merger was complete. While others felt seen and heard, Hector instantly felt stressed.

The week before, Hector had a private meeting with Derek about the upcoming changes in organizational structure, and

Derek asked him about his biggest concerns regarding this shift in the company. Hector talked about how he'd worked hard to consistently hit all the targets and expectations during the past year, but with his recent divorce taking up so much of his mental and emotional space, he wasn't able to achieve the way he had in the past. He'd missed the mark in his sales goals, only hitting about 75 percent of the target this quarter compared to 90 percent in the previous quarter.

The timing of this underperformance couldn't have been worse. With the acquisition looming, Hector feared he'd be first on the chopping block, even though he'd been a consistently high performer before.

Derek reassured him, "Look, I totally understand your worries, and I think the majority of the team is feeling similar fears. You're a good team player, you're always helping out where you can, and everyone has off months. I think they're going to focus on other departments and our sales team should be relatively untouched. Besides that, I'll be sticking up for you and the team, so you can feel good knowing that you've got an advocate on your side."

Hector felt relieved. He was so grateful that Derek understood his concerns and that he wasn't going to be left to defend himself and his worth all on his own. Having a supportive boss could make all the difference, and Hector felt more at ease knowing he wasn't alone.

"That definitely makes me feel better. Thanks, Derek. With this divorce and trying to figure out what's going on with the kids, I just haven't had my usual bandwidth to manage everything like I used to. I really can't afford to not have the stability of this job, because having a stable position could make a huge impact on whether I get joint custody of the kids. Plus, there's just so much fear throughout the company, it's hard to focus. I think a lot of us are bracing for a layoff email from HR, just like other departments have gotten, so it's hard to do our best when we never know when it might be our last day."

Hector left that initial meeting feeling seen, heard, and understood. While he still felt anxious about the future of his team, he felt like he could breathe a little bit more easily. At least he had a boss who knew how to show up for his team and who wanted to do the right thing.

Unfortunately, a week later, Derek disclosed Hector's personal information in the team huddle, sharing Hector's individual fears with the team, and Hector felt worse than ever. He thought the private meeting with Derek was confidential and that his concerns were going to be kept between them, but Derek put him on blast in front of the whole group. Others had no idea that Hector was having performance issues, and he felt so exposed. After sitting with his anger for a bit, Hector realized this went beyond just feeling vulnerable. He felt betrayed.

Hector had thought he could trust Derek, but he questioned whether that was still a wise choice. It's one thing to speak generally to the sentiments of the team, but it's another thing to call him out specifically in front of everyone.

Hector knew he needed to say something—otherwise he would dread coming to work and he wouldn't want to stay on Derek's team even if he didn't get cut. So he scheduled a meeting with Derek for later that week.

The whole week, Hector felt nervous about his upcoming meeting. Derek was in a position of power and had control over whether he stood up for his team if layoffs came down the pike.

Hector knew his saying something could influence Derek's willingness to come to his defense and that he might get put on the chopping block, but he weighed out his options. It was either speak up now or let the resentment brew. Hector's choice was clear.

"Thanks for taking the time to meet today. I know you've got a really busy schedule with everything going on, so I appreciate you fitting me in on short notice. First, I wanted to say that I really appreciated you directly addressing all our fears and concerns. It means a lot to have a leader who cares and who wants to stand up for us. I know a lot of us have never had that experience, so thank you."

Derek smiled and said, "Oh yeah, of course. I think we have to band together during uncertain times, and it's my job as your supervisor to have your best interests in mind. I don't want you all to be stressed, though I know that's pretty much impossible during times like these, but if I can do something to help, I want to do it. Are there other things I can do to help?"

"Well . . . now that you mention it, there is one thing," Hector replied. "In the team huddle, you mentioned that we're all feeling stressed because some of us were unable to hit the sales goals for the quarter, but then you specifically mentioned me and the concerns I brought up to you in our one-on-one meeting a couple of weeks ago. It threw me off because I thought those things were said in confidence, and when you put it out there to the team, it was kind of embarrassing. I'm known as one of the high performers, and I don't want the rest of the team to think I'm slacking or falling behind. I felt put on the spot, and it affected the trust we've built."

Derek's entire demeanor shifted. Hector could visibly see

that Derek had no idea he had said something inappropriate. His intentions were clearly positive, but his impact was negative, and Derek was realizing that in the moment.

"Oh no, I had no idea that I'd said something that was out of pocket. Thank you for sharing this with me. It totally makes sense that you felt embarrassed, put on the spot, and that it was a breach of trust because you shared those fears privately with me and I should have connected the dots to not tell them what you shared. I called out your concerns in front of the team, and it's understandable that you feared it might impact the way the team views you. I'm really sorry that I disclosed your information to the group without your consent, and it won't happen again. I'll make sure to keep our conversations private, and if I plan to share something, I'll get your explicit permission instead of assuming that it's okay."

Derek didn't get defensive, and he didn't try to justify his actions. He took responsibility. Hector felt better knowing that his boss recognized his mistakes. He didn't expect Derek to always get it right, but he was grateful for Derek's accountability. Hector started to feel more trusting of Derek, and with time and consistency, Derek proved that he was worthy of Hector's trust. The relational repair was what Hector needed, and Derek gave it to him.

Mistakes happen. In fact, they are inevitable. Perfection isn't the goal, but you need to learn how to take responsibility for mistakes. And there is a right way to take responsibility.

It's the repair that really counts.

Derek did a few things really well that we can all learn from. He followed what I call the AVP framework. AVP, as mentioned earlier, stands for acknowledge, validate, and plan.

In order to successfully repair after a mistake, you need to acknowledge and name the mistake, validate the other person's feelings and viewpoint, and create a plan for the specific actions you will take to prevent this mistake from occurring again.

Acknowledge

When you make a mistake, the temptation is to explain why you behaved the way you did. You want the other person to understand your intentions and to see that you weren't malicious in your motivations. Even deeper than that is the desire to diffuse blame and reduce shame.

Unfortunately, this is rarely received well. The person on the other end interprets your explanations as excuses, and they feel like you're skirting accountability. They then get defensive because they feel unheard, and it becomes a conversation about whether your good intentions outweigh the negative impact.

Derek could have said that the intention behind sharing Hector's concerns was to help the team feel less alone in their stress and worries about performance, but he didn't. Justifying actions further erodes trust instead of repairing it.

Acknowledging simply requires you to acknowledge the harm the other person has expressed. Even if you disagree with their feelings, what they're experiencing is valid and needs to be understood. Derek took a second to acknowledge that Hector felt put on the spot and that it was a breach of trust. He named the concerns that Hector expressed, and he didn't try to justify why he shared Hector's information with the group.

This acknowledgment allowed Hector to see that Derek

understood what he'd done wrong. Too often, people apologize in a vague way, saying, "I'm sorry for what I did" or "I'm sorry that happened." But what are they actually sorry for? What was it that they did, or what was it that happened? It sounds simple, but being specific about what went wrong shows the other person that you fully understand your misstep, which in turn makes it more likely that you won't make that mistake again.

To do this, you'll want to listen carefully to what the other person is expressing and identify the underlying issue. The person you're speaking with might feel less trusting, but why is that the case? What specific actions did you take that negatively impacted their trust in you? Name these things in the first part of your apology.

Validate

Derek did a good job of validating Hector's concerns, signaling to Hector that his stance was understood. He expressed how Hector's feelings totally made sense, and that his sharing private information with the group would of course constitute a breach of trust.

Hector wanted to be sure Derek understood the emotional impact of his actions. He expressed that he felt embarrassed because being called out in front of the group diminished his reputation. Derek validated Hector's feelings of embarrassment, showing that he understood why sharing that private information would feel embarrassing, as it could impact how others viewed him.

Validating simply entails helping the other person feel

seen, heard, and understood. If someone expresses that they're worried or frustrated, then it's your job to help them not feel crazy or out of bounds for feeling that way. This normalizes their response and shows empathy and compassion for where they're coming from.

Using active listening skills and piecing together the rationale behind the feelings is how you validate someone else's experience.

The phrases below can help acknowledge another person's feelings without you cosigning their feelings. Even if you don't agree with how the other person feels, you can still validate their experience.

Fill in the blanks below with the feelings that the other person is expressing:

- *"I understand why you felt ________."*
- *"That makes sense that you felt ________ when ________ happened."*
- *"Anyone would feel ________ if they were in your position."*
- *"I'm sorry that you felt ________. I know that must be hard."*

This skill is critical not only in moments of repair, but is also applicable to any conversation with a team member. Connection is rooted in understanding, empathy, and compassion, and validation is essential to cultivating connection.

Plan

It's not enough to just acknowledge missteps, validate feelings, and move on. Repair requires a concrete plan that shows forethought in ensuring the issues at hand get resolved. The plan needs to be specific and address the concerns that were brought forth.

Saying "It won't happen again" is hollow because it doesn't provide clarity to the person on the receiving end about how you intend to ensure it won't happen again. In Derek's case, he told Hector that he wouldn't share information discussed in private, and that if he wanted to potentially share something Hector said, he would double-check with Hector first instead of assuming he knew what would be deemed acceptable.

This type of specificity is needed for an effective repair plan. You need to identify action steps that you can take that will result in a different outcome. These action steps should be informed by what's shared in the conversation.

If someone says to you that they're frustrated about not being included in emails going out to the client, even though they're a part of the client team, too, and that their feedback hasn't been incorporated, then just telling them that you'll include them isn't specific enough.

Instead, you could say that you will be sure to CC them on future emails, and that you'll specifically ask for their input in emails going forward so they can contribute to the conversation. These two steps address the pain points of feeling excluded and not feeling like their input is being considered. It's much more effective than just saying you'll include them.

The next time you're apologizing, ask yourself, "What did

this person express that they need from me, and what can I specifically do to ensure that need is met?"

Formulate one or two action steps, and communicate those directly.

Once you've acknowledged, validated, and planned a course of action, then it's time to respond congruently, as we discussed earlier in the CHECK-IN framework. Trust takes time to repair, and it's through congruent, consistent actions that trust is restored.

You might want to speed up the process, but that only gets in the way of repair. There are no shortcuts, only daily actions that prove over time that you are making an effort to do better.

Neurodivergent Tip

The words you use when you're repairing are as important as your plan to prevent future issues.

Debbie and Erika were joking around about how Debbie has some particular ways that she likes to work. Debbie is diagnosed with obsessive compulsive disorder, and Erika pointed out that Debbie needs her workspace to be exactly in order, so much so that every paper needs to be in its place. Debbie chuckled that yes, she is a bit obsessive about her desk and making sure that things are well organized.

Then Erika smirked and said, "It's not just your desk. It's so weird how you go back to check whether your office door is locked a million times. You're always a couple minutes late to our meetings because you just can't get out of there. It's like back and forth, and back and forth. It's hilarious!"

Debbie went from feeling included in the joke to feeling like she was the butt of the joke. She was offended that Erika was making fun of her struggles with compulsions. It's one thing to pick on her overly organized nature, but Debbie experienced debilitating compulsions to check locks, and they negatively impacted her quality of life. She paused and said to Erika, "Hey, I know that some aspects of my disorder are funny, but the lock-checking is a really hard one for me. It takes a lot of time and energy out of my day, and I get really anxious if I don't do it. I know it makes me late to the meetings, but I can't help it. I'd appreciate it if we didn't make fun of that."

Erika paused and retorted, "I'm sorry *if* I hurt your feelings. I was just trying to have fun with you and didn't think it would cause any problems."

The word *if* really bothered Debbie. It was no longer a question of *if* Erika offended her. Debbie directly expressed that it did, in fact, bother her, and Erika saying that she was sorry if she hurt her feelings felt like an invalidation of Debbie's feelings.

Erika's explanation of how she was just "trying to have fun" and how she "didn't think it would cause any problems" made it seem as though Debbie was being too sensitive. Debbie didn't appreciate this language, and Erika's apology felt hollow as a result.

One of the most common mistakes people make, especially with neurodivergent colleagues, is using language that unintentionally dismisses their concerns. They use conditional language and try to justify their actions instead of just acknowledging and validating the harm caused.

The word *if* in apologies invalidates everything that follows. Instead, just say, "I'm sorry that I hurt your feelings by cracking a joke. I appreciate you letting me know that a line was crossed, and I won't make jokes like that again."

This language shift is important for repairing trust with neurodivergent people, but it's also crucial for repairing trust in all of our relationships.

The way that you communicate matters. Be mindful of what you say and how you say it.

In a world where people use neurodivergent diagnoses as colloquialisms, like "The weather is being so bipolar today" or "I'm feeling all over the place; what an ADHD day," it's easy for people to think that it's okay to comment or poke fun. If someone's "jokes" make you feel uncomfortable, then it's not okay and it needs to be addressed.

Try to have a conversation with the person who is making the comments to see if they will stop. If they continue making uncomfortable statements, you might need to escalate to a leader you trust.

You deserve to work in an environment where you feel safe, and boundary crosses impact your emotional safety.

Chapter 13

CHECK-**IN**

INterrupt Discomfort and Stay Present

THE BLANK STARE felt like it was boring a hole into my soul, and I could feel my heart pounding.

"Breathe," I said to myself. "Just breathe."

I had just finished sharing my discontentment with my boss. I didn't feel like I was getting enough support in our one-on-one meetings, and despite giving her this feedback in the past, not much had changed. I had incredibly complex cases in my caseload, including asylees and unaccompanied minors who had endured tremendous trauma, and I needed a listening ear and support.

This boss had a habit of focusing on the documentation and the administrative aspects of the job, which of course are important, but I needed professional guidance about how to best manage the stress and overwhelm of treating children who had been sexually assaulted and abused by the adults who had assisted them in finding safety in the United States.

It was clear that she was uncomfortable with heavy emotional topics, and her focus on the technical aspects of the job was a way to avoid diving into the discomfort of these conversations. However, as one of two people who took on these complex trauma cases, I needed to have a supervisor who understood me and could hold space for me.

When I shared that I felt like I needed more or different support than what I was receiving, she looked like she was frozen. She stared at me like I had spoken in a language she couldn't comprehend. I knew she might need time to process, but this was exactly the type of lack of connection that I was telling her about in that moment.

It was clear to me that her inability to regulate her nervous system and manage her emotional responses was going to continue being problematic at work. If she had the right tools to interrupt the discomfort she felt during difficult conversations, then maybe the outcome could be different.

My boss's reaction is all too common. Many people clam up or avoid difficult conversations at work because having those types of discussions can feel overwhelming or make them feel anxious. The result is disconnection and misunderstandings, which negatively impact team dynamics. The person on the receiving end walks away feeling as though they're too much or did something wrong, when in reality, the appropriate response would be to be with them as they express their feelings to you.

Interrupting discomfort requires you to practice and master the skills of emotional regulation that you learned earlier in this book. Recognizing your physiological response during difficult conversations, including the increase in heart rate, jitteriness, sweaty palms, and temptation to shut down, is key because the desire to avoid can sneak up on you.

Being able to take a moment to calm down and stay present ensures that you're in tune with the person you're speaking with versus being distant and thinking of how to get out of the conversation. Remember, calm body = calm mind. Use four-seven-eight breathing, the five senses grounding, and other grounding techniques to combat the tendency to lean away instead of leaning in.

One of the other most common exit strategies during difficult conversations is platitudes and toxic positivity.

You might be tempted to say things like "It's not that big of a deal," "It'll get better," or "Don't worry about it," but this is another form of avoidance. You may be well intentioned, but toxic positivity is a way to bypass the challenging emotions the other person is experiencing. It invalidates their experience, because if it was so simple to just not worry about the issue at hand, they wouldn't be worrying about it in the first place. It's another form of trying to fix the problem, which is usually not what people need in their interpersonal interactions. Remember, if they wanted your advice or for you to make it better, they'd ask you for that.

Once you're able to get to a place where you can ride the wave of discomfort and stay with people in their pain and difficulties, you'll find that your interactions go much more smoothly. People will feel like they can trust you and share with you without the worry that it won't be well received or will be received with judgment.

You might be thinking that this sounds intense and that you're not anyone's therapist. While that's true, being able to stay calm and be present with people is a skill that is not just reserved for therapists. You can participate in challenging conversations while still maintaining your boundaries because you're not trying to resolve or process the issue at hand. Instead, view interrupting your discomfort as a critical component of emotional and relational intelligence, which is what everyone needs to be successful in the workplace.

We're no longer viewing emotional intelligence, relational intelligence, and emotional regulation as soft skills. We need to view them as essential skills for success.

Neurodivergent Tip

The CHECK-IN framework is a valuable tool to utilize with your neurodivergent colleagues because it focuses on providing support that is in alignment with the individual's unique needs. It's a framework that requires you to adapt and attune versus assuming that what works for one person will work for another.

When I spoke with Victor about what was most helpful for him while he was struggling to cope with the complex post-traumatic stress resulting from childhood abuse and compounded by a horrific car accident, he said that he most valued the fact that his work teams listened and didn't try to tell him what to do. They interrupted the discomfort they felt with him sharing his pain and focused on what he needed instead.

His family and friends had tons of unsolicited advice for what types of physical therapy, emotional therapy, and insurance help he needed. They felt uncomfortable with the fact that Victor would be experiencing pain long term, so they tried their best to fix it as a way to reduce their own discomfort.

To his surprise, his work team ended up being the ones who listened and understood him the most. They didn't try to prescribe solutions; they instead showed empathy and compassion for his circumstances.

He also appreciated that people asked him what would be most helpful. He struggled to know what types of supports were available at work while he was having frequent doctors' appointments and therapy appointments, so having a menu of options made a difference and reduced the decision fatigue that he was already feeling from having to manage so much at one time.

Because of the fear of driving that developed after the car accident, Victor's boss offered to allow him to work from home indefinitely once he was in a place to work again. The avoidance was a symptom of his post-traumatic stress disorder (PTSD) following the accident, and his boss understood that forcing him to come into the office was counterproductive.

His team was willing to take on some of his clients while he recovered, they were happy to step in to share his work during meetings so he wouldn't have to attend, and they donated their time off so he could properly recover, because much of his paid time off was eaten up while he was in the hospital. Victor found all these options helpful and was so grateful that his team was ready to support him on the long road to getting well again.

Too often, we're used to carrying the burden of our struggles alone because people in the past have invalidated our neurodivergence and viewed it as a barrier to performing our best at work. They've told us to push through and that we should learn how to operate like neurotypical folks. We think that we have to figure it out on our own, and we may hesitate to accept support because we view it as a weakness.

Victor's story highlights the importance of leaders and colleagues providing options for support, but he's also an example of accepting help when it's offered. Don't try to just grin and bear it; set yourself up for success by utilizing the resources available to you. If a workplace isn't willing to give you reasonable accommodations, even though legally they're required to go through a reasonable accommodations process, then that's not a place you'll want to continue working.

One of the most important takeaways from this book is that neurodivergent folks are not a monolith. Using the CHECK-IN framework allows you to tune in to what each person you interact with needs so you can accommodate them accordingly. Don't assume that everyone with ADHD can't focus, that everyone with depression can't function, or that everyone with PTSD is incapacitated.

Asking the right questions illuminates the answers for what people need at work, and meeting them where they are is a conduit for connection.

Chapter 14

When You Are Working Well, Everything Works Well

THE EMPLOYEES GAZED up at the numbers with tears streaming down their cheeks. They couldn't believe what they were seeing. Their lives were changing right before their eyes.

A few years prior, Pete Stavros, the owner of an investment firm named KKR, made the decision to invest in a company called C.H.I. Overhead Doors. Before Pete took over, only eighteen people had stock in the company, which meant only eighteen people were able to build wealth. Everyone else was paid a low wage and struggled to make ends meet. Given that the company was located in Amish country in central Illinois, intergenerational wealth was hard to come by.

After Stavros took over, all eight hundred employees were given stock and ownership in the company. As the value of the company rose, so did their wealth. They each became stakeholders, and they now started to pave a pathway toward achieving the type of financial stability they had only dreamed of.

Before Stavros started to transform the organizational culture, employee satisfaction and engagement were dismal. Employees did not feel as though they had a voice or that their opinions mattered. They refused to complete employee surveys, and they stopped investing their energy in improving the organization. Outcomes suffered.

Stavros took a different approach. He attuned to the needs of his employees and not only gave them a financial stake in the business, but gave them a voice, too. He realized that his teams didn't just want to come to work to earn a paycheck; they wanted to work for a company that was aligned with their values and their vision.

Each quarter, the entire company came together to openly talk about what was working and what wasn't. Stavros shared financial information transparently, and he included the employees in business decisions. They weren't just cogs in the machine; they were creating the machine.

He provided the employees with an annual budget of one million dollars to invest in the workplace. They came up with ideas for what they wanted to add, and they decided how they would allocate the funds to make these improvements. The employees would vote and come to a consensus as a group.

This led to significant improvements within the workplace. For example, one year the employees voted for new break rooms where the staff could enjoy their downtime, and another year they voted to add a cafeteria so people could have a healthy meal while at work. In a different year, they voted to add a health and wellness clinic in order to improve access to health care. Each year provided a new opportunity for the employees to decide what they needed and for them to act on it.

Stavros describes it as not only giving employees a voice, but also allowing them to see their voice manifest in tangible results.

These shifts didn't just benefit the employees; the outcomes improved as well. Productivity skyrocketed, waste and scrap decreased, and employees were better able to respond to client needs. The company gained market share as a result and became worth ten times what it had been worth a few years prior.

Eventually, it came time for Stavros and KKR to sell the company. He gathered all the employees in a room and shared the news. He reminded them that their jobs were safe, and that they could now see on the screen before them how their stock in the company grew during his years of ownership. The numbers flew up and kept increasing. Some earned one and a half times their annual income. Others earned two and a half, three and a half, four and a half times their annual income. The most tenured employees earned six and a half times their yearly income. Some of the truck drivers made eight hundred thousand dollars. This was a life-altering amount of money that would not only give these employees and their families financial security, but also would allow them to pass down this wealth for generations to come.

As the employees saw the numbers, tears flowed and hugs were shared all around because they knew their lives were forever changed. These employees earned these results with their hard work and dedication, and the community benefited, as $340 million were invested into the local economy, improving schools and bringing more businesses to the region.

Stavros and C.H.I. Overhead Doors' story is an example of

what is possible. They are the ultimate example of how attunement can transform workplaces.

When leaders and organizations tune in to what teams really desire, outcomes improve. When they invest in their employees, results skyrocket. When employees feel like they have a voice, culture transforms. When teams feel connected and driven toward a common goal, magic happens.

Attuning to colleagues, teams, and organizations is how we create happy, healthy workplaces where people thrive. It's the secret sauce to a successful workplace. It's what's been missing from so many companies and why so many people have become disillusioned with work.

But the hopeful news is that it can change. Right now, today, it can change. We can all be a part of the culture shift toward a workplace that makes us feel valued, cared for, and understood. We can learn these skills, share this knowledge, and practice connecting in a way that builds bridges instead of widening gaps.

It's not a question of whether attunement can make a difference. It does make a difference, and Stavros's story, which was featured in his TED Talk from TED2024, is the exemplar.[1]

Attunement is good for business, it's good for the bottom line, and it's good for humanity. We just have to make the conscious decision to be a part of challenging the norms.

The question is: Will you join me in becoming a culture changemaker? If so, then start applying all that you've learned. Unlearn, learn, and relearn. And if you feel so inspired, share this book with someone else so we can create a movement together.

Acknowledgments

"If you want to go fast, go alone; if you want to go far, go together." —African proverb

The people in my community have helped me go much farther than I ever could have dreamed. There are so many people to thank and only a couple of pages to do it in, so here goes.

First and foremost, thank YOU for reading and sharing this book with everyone who would benefit. A book can't be successful without readers like you.

To my husband, Alan, who continues to be the best partner I could ask for. We've been together for almost twenty years, and you have always encouraged me to follow my dreams. From reading my entire book from start to finish and giving me feedback before the manuscript was due so I could submit the best version possible, to being my business manager who accompanies me on my speaking engagements around the world, to rubbing my back and hearing me vent about my anxieties, you are proof that true, unconditional love exists.

As immigrants, my mom and dad came to the US with five hundred dollars in their pockets and turned it into the

American Dream. My mom is a highly educated woman with three degrees who had to start over in the US as a grocery store clerk, and eventually made her way to the top as a VP with Bank of America. She showed me that you can overcome anything if you put your mind to it. My dad came here with two master's degrees and still faced discrimination when trying to provide for us. They are my examples of resilience. Thank you for sacrificing everything you built in India so that we could live our best lives here. Dad, *Working Well* is being released on your 75th birthday, which I think is probably a good omen of sorts, and I smile every time I see your excitement. Thank you, Mom and Dad, for supporting me and for being the first to brag about me to the aunties and uncles. My sister, Shruti, brother-in-law, Shamik, and nephew and niece, Roshan and Ayana, have been cheerleaders for me. My sister encouraged me to become a therapist, and she's always had my back, advocating for me to pursue my dreams despite the expectation to follow the traditional path of becoming a doctor, lawyer, or engineer. Everyone gave me feedback about the book covers, and Rosh and Yanu say my next book should be a children's book (we'll see!). My cousins, aunts, and uncles have rooted for me as they follow my journey, too, even though they're thousands of miles away in India, Canada, and Europe.

While they're no longer on this physical plane, my grandparents, Dadaji (whose story you've heard), Dadiji, Nana, and Nani would be so proud to see this book come to life. They always relished my success, and I can feel their loving presence.

To Amy Cuddy, my friend and mentor (friendtor), who graciously said yes to writing my foreword, thank you. Thank you for believing in me, thank you for giving me the gift of your guidance, and thank you for writing your first foreword *ever* for me. I'm immensely grateful for your pep talks, the way you softly but honestly keep it real, and for encouraging me as an author and speaker. Sometimes I feel behind, and you remind me that I'm exactly where I need to be.

My framily (friend-family) kept me grounded through all of this.

To my best friend, Sarah Harper, you have always motivated me to pursue my wildest dreams, and when I'm surprised they come true, you remind me that I was a badass all along and you knew I could do it. I'm thankful we met in graduate school and are still close friends a decade later. Jen Rose, whom I adore, you've been a sounding board for me all along. From the daily voice notes back and forth, to helping me release control and expectations when needed, you've reminded me to enjoy the journey instead of focusing on the destination. Jolie Miller, thank you for advocating for me to become a LinkedIn Learning Instructor and for reminding me of my worth. We became friends during a tough time, but your friendship is incredibly meaningful to me. Chris Do, thank you for being my friend and for seeing my potential back in those Clubhouse years. You've taught me how to stand in my power as a speaker, author, and entrepreneur, and I appreciate how you nudge me to see how far I've come. Denise Hamilton, back in 2020, you inspired me to become a professional speaker, advocated for me, and were a source of support when I couldn't see the next step ahead. I appreciate you immensely. Billy Samoa Saleeby, you're the best hype person and I'm grateful to have you as a friend and collaborator. Our visit to the Magic Castle will always be one of my fondest memories, and your ability to connect and show care is ummatched. Franny Hogi, thank you for planting the seeds with me bring this book to fruition. You showed me that it was much more doable than I thought at the start of 2024. Judy Molina, you've always helped me grow as a clinician, and you're a trusted confidant, sister. Thank you, my love. Kasley Killam, thank you for advocating for me, advising me, and encouraging me to let my dreams unfold. Your wisdom is invaluable. Michele Zehr, our jam sessions, deep conversations, and "Bella Ruth Naperstack" jokes have always uplifted me. Aaron Daniels, thank you for reminding me that success requires investment, and that the payoffs are worth it. Crystal Armes, I appreciate your supporting every milestone; thanks for rallying.

To my TED family, specifically Kelly Stoetzel, Raven White, Cyndi Stivers, Keryn Gottshalk, Nicole Darsney, and Sabina Osorio, thank you for being a part of my transformation from therapist to thought leader.

Kelly, you brought me into the TED community back in 2022, and my life hasn't been the same since. Thank you for being my friend and a mentor to me as I grow and expand. I always look forward to our Zoom catch-ups! Raven, I'm thankful for your friendship. You've held space for me during some difficult moments, and being a part of the Ignite Program is such a joy. I appreciate your supporting me, my ideas, and my dreams. Cyndi, your friendship and mentorship are invaluable. Your advocacy, expert feedback on my covers, and encouragement through the book process have aided me in knowing the best path forward. Keryn and Nicole, thank you for inviting me to lead Discovery Sessions at TEDWomen and TEDNext. Nothing lights me up more than facilitating transformation in real time. Sabina, our conversations are always so much deeper than small talk, and I love that I'm top of mind for sharing the gift that is TED with the world as a TED Ambassador.

Ann Shoket and The Li.st, thank you for sharing your tips and tricks for making this book a success. The advice from *New York Times* bestselling authors was incredibly impactful, and I appreciate being in a supportive community with you all.

And last but certainly not least, thank you to my team. You've been instrumental in bringing this book to life, and I couldn't have done it without you.

To my editors at Penguin Random House/Tarcher, Lauren Appleton and Sabrey Manning, I've appreciated your insights and patience throughout the birthing of this book. Your feedback shaped this into an approachable, practical way to live and work better. Paula Stone Williams, my speaking coach, thank you for opening so many doors for me. When I wasn't sure about where to go next, you showed me the way. To Jonathan Merritt, my agent, and the Christopher Ferebee team, thank you for taking a chance on me and seeing the potential in my book. Jonathan, you were my biggest advocate, you were my late-night anxiety text buddy (millennials never sleep), and you were able to assuage my fears throughout the process. Thank you, Dr. Mallory McCord, for helping me conduct our first-to-market research study on attunement at work. I know the results will help shape the future of how we work. Thanks to Fortier PR for working so hard to get this message out there, and thanks to Outspoken Agency for also elevating my message through my speaking.

If I forgot anyone because I didn't have enough space, know that you're in my heart and you're appreciated.

Notes

Introduction: From Discord to Harmony

1 "New APA Poll: One in Three Americans Feels Lonely Every Week," January 30, 2024, American Psychiatric Association, https://www.psychiatry.org/news-room/news-releases/new-apa-poll-one-in-three-americans-feels-lonely-e.

Chapter 1: The Science of Attunement

1 Uri Hasson, Yuval Nir, Ifat Levy, Galit Fuhrmann, and Rafael Malach, "Intersubject Synchronization of Cortical Activity During Natural Vision," *Science* 303, no. 5664 (March 12, 2004): 1634–40, https://doi.org/10.1126/science.1089506.

2 Alejandro Pérez, Manuel Carreiras, and Jon Andoni Duñabeitia, "Brain-to-Brain Entrainment: EEG Interbrain Synchronization While Speaking and Listening," *Scientific Reports* 7 (June 23, 2017): 4190, https://doi.org/10.1038/s41598-017-04464-4.

3 Pauline Pérez, Jens Madsen, Leah Banellis, Başak Türker, et al., "Conscious Processing of Narrative Stimuli Synchronizes Heart Rate between Individuals," *Cell Reports* 36, no. 11 (September 14, 2021): 109692, https://doi.org/10.1016/j.celrep.2021.109692.

4 Daniel J. Siegel, MD, "Interpersonal Neurobiology," Dr. Dan Siegel—An Introduction to Interpersonal Neurobiology, accessed June 11, 2025, https://drdansiegel.com/interpersonal-neurobiology.

5 Daniel J. Siegel, MD, "Mindsight: A Skill That Can Change Your Brain," Mindsight—Dr. Dan Siegel, accessed June 16, 2025, https://drdansiegel.com/mindsight.

6 Siegel, "Mindsight."

Chapter 2: Mirrors and Models: Reflecting on Your Childhood Relationships

1 Andrea M. Scheetz and Timothy J. Fogarty, "Walking the Talk: Enacted Ethical Climates as Psychological Contract Venues for Potential Whistleblowers," *Journal of Accounting & Organizational Change* 15, no. 4 (November 22, 2019): 654–77, https://doi.org/10.1108/JAOC-06-2018-0047.

2 Thomas Olesen, "The Politics of Whistleblowing in Digitalized Societies," *Politics & Society* 47, no. 2 (June 2019): 277–97, https://doi.org/10.1177/0032329219844140.

3 Sokol Loci and Judita Peterlin, "Leadership Development Elements Contained in the Life Stories of Leadership Members," *SAGE Open* 13, no. 4 (November 2023): 1–13. https://doi.org/10.1177/21582440231210774.

Chapter 3: Reacting Versus Responding: Understanding Triggers and Reactions

1 Raabia Sattar, Rebecca Lawton, Gillian Janes, Mai Elshehaly, et al., "A Systematic Review of Workplace Triggers of Emotions in the Healthcare Environment, the Emotions Experienced, and the Impact on Patient Safety," *BMC Health Services Research* 24, no. 1 (May 9, 2024): 603, https://doi.org/10.1186/s12913-024-11011-1.

Chapter 4: Know Thyself + Keep Calm and Carry On

1 Michelle Yarwood, "James-Lange Theory," in *Psychology of Human Emotion: An Open Access Textbook*, chapter 2, Penn State–powered Pressbooks, accessed June 16, 2025, https://psu.pb.unizin.org/psych425/chapter/james-lange-theory.

2 Edward F. Pace-Schott, Marlissa C. Amole, Tatjana Aue, Michela Balconi, et al., "Physiological Feelings," *Journal of Psychophysiology* 33, no. 2 (May 22, 2019): 67–81, https://doi.org/10.1027/0269-8803/a000246.

3 Daniel J. Siegel, "Dan Siegel: Name it to Tame it," YouTube video, December 8, 2014, https://www.youtube.com/watch?v=ZcDLzppD4Jc.

4 “In Pictures: 10 All-Time Great CEO Outbursts,” *Forbes*, July 10, 2009, https://www.forbes.com/2009/07/10/ceo-anger-management-ceonetwork-leadership-outbursts_slide.html.

5 “In Pictures: 10 All-Time Great CEO Outbursts,” *Forbes*.

6 Hector P. Madrid, “Emotion Regulation, Positive Affect, and Promotive Voice Behavior at Work,” *Frontiers in Psychology* 11 (July 2020): 1739, https://doi.org/10.3389/fpsyg.2020.01739.

7 Madrid, “Emotion Regulation, Positive Affect, and Promotive Voice Behavior at Work.”

8 Jaruwan Vierra, Orachorn Boonla, and Piyapong Prasertsri, “Effects of Sleep Deprivation and 4-7-8 Breathing Control on Heart Rate Variability, Blood Pressure, Blood Glucose, and Endothelial Function in Healthy Young Adults,” *Physiological Reports* 10, no. 13 (July 13, 2022): e15389, https://doi.org/10.14814/phy2.15389.

9 Mark Travers, “A Psychologist Shares the ‘90-Second Rule’ to Survive Emotional Waves,” *Forbes*, March 10, 2025, https://www.forbes.com/sites/traversmark/2025/03/10/a-psychologist-shares-the-90-second-rule-to-survive-emotional-waves.

Chapter 5: The Connection Gap

1 Julia Pryce and Kelsey Deane, "The Mentor Attunement Scale: A Tool to Measure a Critical Mentoring Skill-Set," *Mentoring & Tutoring: Partnership in Learning* 33, no. 1 (November 6, 2024): 95–111, https://doi.org/10.1080/13611267.2024.2420122.

2 Amy Edmondson, "Psychological Safety and Learning Behavior in Work Teams," *Administrative Science Quarterly* 44, no. 2 (1999): 350–83, https://web.mit.edu/curhan/www/docs/Articles/15341_Readings/Group_Performance/Edmondson%20Psychological%20safety.pdf.

3 Michael Housman and Dylan Minor, "Toxic Workers," Working Paper No. 16-057 (Harvard Business School, October 2015, revised November 2015), https://www.hbs.edu/ris/Publication%20Files/16-057_d45c0b4f-fa19-49de-8f1b-4b12fe054fea.pdf.

4 "New Research Exposes the Hidden Costs of 'Toxic Employees,'" Cornerstone OnDemand, March 31, 2015, https://www.cornerstoneondemand.com/company/news-room/press-releases/new-research-exposes-hidden-costs-toxic-employees.

5 Sarah Wells, "Exploring the Dangers of AI in Mental Health Care," Stanford Institute for Human-Centered Artificial Intelligence, June 11, 2025, https://hai.stanford.edu/news/exploring-the-dangers-of-ai-in-mental-health-care.

6 Frank Landymore, "CEO Brags That He Gets 'Extremely Excited' Firing People and Replacing Them with AI," *Futurism,* July 25, 2025, https://futurism.com/ceo-replacing-workers-ai.

7 Charles Daly, "Klarna Turns from AI to Real Person Customer Service," Bloomberg News, May 8, 2025, https://www.bloomberg.com/news/articles/2025-05-08/klarna-turns-from-ai-to-real-person-customer-service.

8 Craig Hale, "Over Half of UK Businesses Who Replaced Workers with AI Regret Their Decision," *TechRadar Pro,* April 29, 2025, https://www.techradar.com/pro/over-half-of-uk-businesses-who-replaced-workers-with-ai-regret-their-decision.

9 Shubham Agarwal, "AI Isn't Ready to Do Your Job," *Business Insider,* April 22, 2025, https://www.businessinsider.com/ai-agents-study-company-run-by-ai-disaster-replace-jobs-2025-4.

Chapter 6: Trustless Teams

1 Cherylann Mollan, "Yes Madam: Anger after Indian Start-Up Pretends to Sack Stressed Staff," BBC News, December 11, 2024, https://www.bbc.com/news/articles/cd0en3nrxpyo.

2 Sydney Lake, "Ex-Cloudflare Employee Records Her Firing and Sparks a Debate about Whether It Was a Layoff

in Disguise or Her Fault," *Fortune*, January 12, 2024, https://fortune.com/2024/01/12/cloudflare-employee-firing-tiktok-layoff-disguise.

3 Monica Sager, "Party City Abruptly Shutting Down All Stores: What We Know," *Newsweek*, December 20, 2024, https://www.newsweek.com/party-city-closing-stores-out-business-2004421.

4 Emmy Abbassi and Jordan Valinsky, "Party City Is Going out of Business," CNN, December 20, 2024, https://www.cnn.com/2024/12/20/business/party-city-shut-down.

5 Amy C. Edmondson, "Managing the Risk of Learning: Psychological Safety in Work Teams," Working Paper No. 02-062 (Harvard Business School, March 2002), https://www.hbs.edu/ris/Publication%20Files/02-062_0b5726a8-443d-4629-9e75-736679b870fc.pdf.

Chapter 7: Managing Well

1 Ashton Jackson, "Nintendo CEO Once Halved Salary to Prevent Layoffs, and It Worked—Why That's So Uncommon Today," CNBC, February 13, 2024, https://www.cnbc.com/2024/02/13/nintendo-ceo-once-halved-salary-to-prevent-layoffs-why-thats-uncommon.html.

2 J. P. Cavanaugh, "A Century of Chef Boy-Ar-Dee," *J. P.'s Blog*, August 16, 2024, https://jpcavanaugh.com/2024/08/16/a-century-of-chef-boy-ar-dee.

3 Catalyst, "Empathic Leaders Drive Employee Engagement and Innovation," news release, September 14, 2021, https://www.catalyst.org/about/newsroom/2021/empathic-leaders-drive-employee-engagement.

4 Sideways 6, "The Top 50 Listening Leaders," *Ideas from Anywhere* (blog), November 22, 2019, https://ideas.sideways6.com/article/the-top-50-listening-leaders.

5 Sideways 6, "The Top 50 Listening Leaders."

Chapter 8: CHECK-IN: Connect

1 Brené Brown, "Research," Brené Brown, accessed June 16, 2025, https://www.brenebrown.com/the-research.

Chapter 11: CHECK-IN: Congruently Respond

1 Nils Hossli, Martin Natter, and René Algesheimer, "On the Importance of Congruence between Personal and Work Values—How Value Incongruence Affects Job Satisfaction: A Multiple Mediation Model," *International Journal of Wellbeing* 14, no. 3 (October 2024): 1–18, https://doi.org/10.5502/ijw.v14i3.2905.

Chapter 12: CHECK-IN: Know How to Repair

1 Mike Isaac, "Inside Uber's Aggressive, Unrestrained Workplace Culture," *The New York Times*, February 22, 2017, https://www.nytimes.com/2017/02/22/technology/uber-workplace-culture.html.

2 Sheelah Kolhatkar, "At Uber, a New C.E.O. Shifts Gears," *The New Yorker*, April 9, 2018.

Chapter 14: When You Are Working Well, Everything Works Well

1 Pete Stavros, "The Secret Ingredient of Business Success," TED Talk, April 2024, video, 13:03, https://www.ted.com/talks/pete_stavros_the_secret_ingredient_of_business_success.

Index

About the Author

Nidhi Tewari, MSW, LCSW, is a licensed therapist and in-demand speaker best known for her work in strengthening workplace culture, connection, and communication. She specializes in applying the latest research to shift the way that companies approach well-being, team cohesion, job satisfaction, and retention.

She is the CEO of Work Well, Live Well, and her clients have included companies like LinkedIn, Warner Brothers Discovery, Molson Coors Beverage Company, NPR, Godiva, McCain Foods, and more. She has also presented at the World Economic Forum, TEDWomen, TEDNext, and Cannes Lions.

Her work has been featured in *The New York Times, Forbes, The Washington Post, Oprah Daily, HuffPost,* and Thrive Global. Her work culture content has reached millions of people across TikTok, LinkedIn, and Instagram.

In her downtime, Nidhi loves traveling, hiking, and finding the best restaurants to indulge in with her husband. She is a proud auntie to her niece and nephew, and she loves the auntie life. She also played the drums in a heavy metal band for half a decade, and still loves getting behind the kit.